Enid Byford has spent the last two years doing the research for *Somerset Pub Walks*, walking widely throughout the county so as to find routes that would combine the best of Somerset's landscape with a fine selection of pubs. Her books include *Somerset Curiosities* and *Somerset Murders*, and she knows the county well.

Enid Byford has had several careers – as a librarian (for which she trained upon leaving school), as a teacher of English in a Nigerian school, as a freelance writer/photographer in Singapore and Canada, and as an editor – the last ten of seventeen years in Ottawa were as the managing editor of *Canadian Geographic*. Since returning with her late husband to Somerset at the beginning of 1984 she has worked as a freelance editor/proof reader and writer.

Dunster, the Yarn Market

SOMERSET
PUB WALKS

ENID BYFORD

Drawings by Louise Dobbs
Maps by Angela Ewing

THE DOVECOTE PRESS

None of these walks takes longer than 2 ½ hours, most take about an hour. The maps are for guide purposes only and not to scale. Whilst all the information about both the walks and pubs was correct at the time of publication, it must be realised that pubs and their menus can change, as can footpath routes.

First published in 1993 by The Dovecote Press Ltd
Stanbridge, Wimborne, Dorset BH21 4JD

ISBN 1 874336 14 8

Printed and bound by Biddles Ltd
Guildford and King's Lynn

Contents

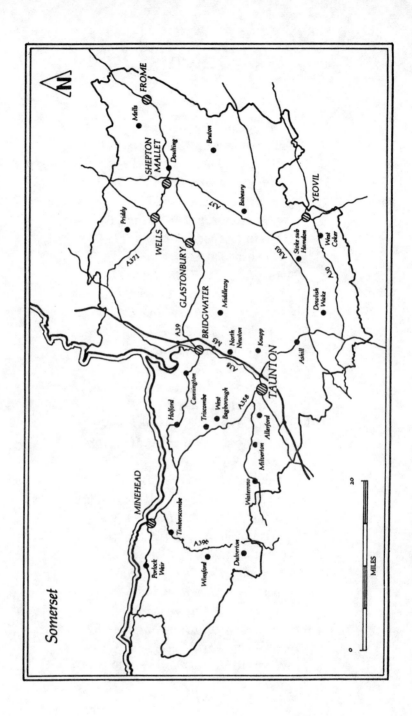

Somerset

Allerford, *Victory Inn*

The Victory is not marked on the 1:25000 map, despite being built as a hostelry in 1730, so to reach it you'll need to make for Norton Fitzwarren on the Barnstaple road out of Taunton. As you leave the village, turn left at the Allerford sign (this hamlet rarely warrants a mention on road maps, and is not to be confused with the Allerford near Minehead). At the T-junction turn left, cross the railway and the Victory is on your left. Behind the inn is part of the long defunct Grand Western Canal, opened in 1838 to link Taunton with Tiverton. The coming of the railway in 1867 eventually killed the canal, but while it was under construction, the navvies patronised the Victory, and later on bargemen used it.

This pub is worth visiting if only for the number of real ales it carries (and at a lower price than many other places); among the twelve are Brains SA, Tangle Foot, Boddingtons and Flowers Original. The food is reasonably priced, well cooked and generous in portion. There's an 'eat as much as you wish' cold counter with a set price; the menu offers interesting items such as pancake filled with salmon and prawns topped by sliced mushrooms and cheese, steak with different sauces, duck with honey sauce, vegetarian fare and various desserts including wonderful Swiss ice creams.

Free House   Licensee: Nick Pike
Tel: (0823) 461282   O/S Ref: 1725

Parking: the pub has a large car park.

Your walk will take just over two hours and leads over fields and alongside the river. Not recommended in wet weather. Begin by crossing the road into the field that lies beside the railway line. Skirt the line until the middle of the second field where there's access for crossing the track by a stile. Keep left to reach a gate, turn right and follow the field at the top to the left, and pass through a gate onto the road. Ahead is Knapp Farm.

Turn left for a short distance to a gate marked Mayfield; follow the path and at the bottom of the slope turn right in front of a house, pass through gate and, keeping to the left, follow a most attractive stream as it meanders alongside a field. Not far beyond where field and stream part company is a gate, pass through and make across the field (or around the edge if the path hasn't been redefined by walkers) to a stile near a cluster of white buildings – this is Court Farm. Turn right up the metalled lane and then left at the fork (Court Farm Pianos). Turn right at the piano factory (keeping it on your left) and through the gate. Please make sure this gate is fastened behind you. Cross the field to the right, go through a kissing gate, carry straight along the lane and you'll come to Hillfarrance Holy Cross Church. Dating to the 16th century, it's a pretty little building, well used and well cared for.

Leaving the church, turn left along the Oake road; to your left is The Bungalow, once the Methodist Chapel. A few yards further at St Brelades take the track beside it (left), cross the stream, turn slightly left and follow the path between a garden wall and a building. Turn right, then left into a field, cross in a slightly left diagonal to another bridge over a stile. The map shows two paths, one along the right boundary, and the other straight across the field, but as it was newly planted I kept to the right and followed the boundaries. Where the path should have crossed into the next field proved difficult to find and to reach the marked path I had to go through the hedge at the end of the field. If you prefer, go on the right track out to the Oake/Bradford

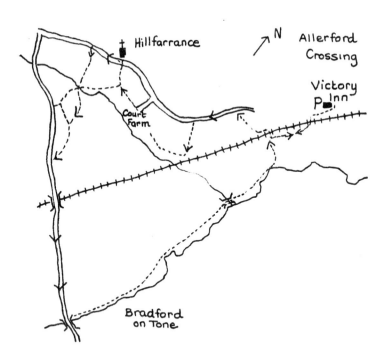

road (you'll join that road if you decide to brave the hedge, anyway). Otherwise, follow the field boundary up the hill, through a gate and across another field to Lang's Farm. On the road, turn left and walk for about 15 minutes towards Bradford.

When you reach the river, turn left before the bridge, and follow the well-defined path for about half-an-hour. For most of the way it skirts the river. The weir is where Bradford Mills once operated (the building is still occupied, but is now a riding school). At the second footbridge, the path divides; take the right path (still along the river), and after passing into the next field (an electricity pylon stands near the boundary), cross to the left and over the stile. Turn right and make for the Victory a field away. You'll pass the overgrown banks and bed of another section of the Grand Western Canal.

Ashill, *Square and Compass Inn*

To reach this pub you'll need to turn off the bypass at the Ashill sign and double back to Windmill Hill near the garage. The pub is run by a young and enthusiastic couple who have worked hard and successfully to make it popular despite being well away from a main road. Of uncertain age, the place was at one time a cider house, was rebuilt in its present state in the 1930s and renovated in 1985. Accommodation is not available, but there is a caravan site behind the pub and camping.

A blackboard displays an imaginative list of dishes, including starters of tomato, apple and celery soup or a mixed salami platter, followed by salmon fillet with a prawn and cream sauce, steak and oyster pie or a lamb and watercress bake, with curried nut loaf or Mediterranean style stuffed aubergine for vegetarians. The printed menu lists items such as deep fried jacket slices served with a choice of dips, deep fried coated Brie with gooseberry dip - and locally made sausages, eggs and chips. Sunday lunches are a speciality, and you're advised to book in advance if you decide to come on a Sunday.

This pub offers real ales, Bass, Flowers, Exmoor and Boddington's bitter, along with draught Guinness.

While having your meal, glance at the field opposite; known as Fighting Field, this was where a troop of rebels, out scouting the Sunday before the Battle of Sedgemoor were engaged by the King's troops led by young Captain Churchill (later Duke of Marlborough) in a skirmish, known then as the Battle of Ashill. Four men died, one lies in St Mary's churchyard, the others were buried elsewhere.

Free Parking   Licensees: Simon and Ginny Reeves
Tel: (0823) 480467   O/S Ref: ST 3116

Parking: you may leave your car at the pub while you walk.

This is a walk for early to mid Spring, when the day is sunny and there has been a spell of dry weather. It will take 1½ hours and leads over gently rolling fields and along quiet lanes, with splendid views to the Blackdown and Quantock Hills. Turn right out of the car park, right again and follow along the lane, ignoring the right hand lane, until you reach the Equestrian Centre, then take the track left, squeeze through the post beside the yellow arrowed gate on the left. Walk to the stile along the right side of the field and follow the left path alongside the hedge. Go downhill until you see a gap in the hedge and cross into the next field. Keep right around the edge of the field until you reach an arrowed stile. Keep left on this next field, pass through the gate in the middle of the far boundary and uphill by the felled oaks. Follow alongside the tatty wire fence to your left, and an orchard, and up the steps to the gate into the churchyard.

It's worth visiting St Mary's Church. Near the path

leading to the north porch is a large tomb containing the remains of Thomas Harvey who died in 1601. Not only is this the oldest remaining tomb in the churchyard, but it is thought the top is the original altar table removed by order of Edward VI following his father's Reformation. Incidentally, it is likely that this Harvey was the father of the Thomas Harvey who left Ashill for New England in 1636 and who founded the town of Taunton, Mass. Inside the church are various monuments, including one dated 1813 to the wife of Thomas Delany Hall of Round Hill, Jamaica.No mention of why the lady should be commemorated at Ashill, but it would seem that her husband was sufficiently sure of himself and his place in the world to feel no explanation was necessary. Above the door leading to the belfry is a delightful modern engraved glass window, known locally as The Joyful Madonna, showing a mother carrying her child across a nearby' field (more of that later). Look also at the 29 shields high on the nave walls – these were put up in the 15th century and, interspersed with flower tablets, display arms of Lords of the Manor of Ashill. Close examination showed them to be carved in the roof timbers; they are unique to this church. Over the door by which you entered is an example of a 'green man'.

When you leave the church take the path through the churchyard, skirting the back gardens of some modern bungalows. Climb the stile and walk left uphill until you reach the path waymarked 'Thickthorn Lane'. Climb the stile, and follow the direction of the arrow. While walking along this section I met a gentleman exercising his dog. We conversed for a few minutes and it transpired that he was Chester Read, the artist who had engraved the window in the belfry; his daughter and his first grandchild were the models. Such meetings with fellow walkers add to the pleasure of being out in the open air.

But back to our walk. Make for the footbridge at the

corner of the field, closed off by an easily opened 'gate' made of chicken wire, and at the other side by a piece of metal. Keep right and ignore the gap in the hedge, climb the stile in the corner of the field, and soon after negotiating the next one beside a bungalow you'll reach Thickthorn Lane. Turn right here and this leads along a quiet surfaced road, massed with flowers in the hedgerow. Ignore the right turn and continue for a few minutes until you reach Windmill Hill Lane. Turn right and the Square and Compass is a few yards along on the right.

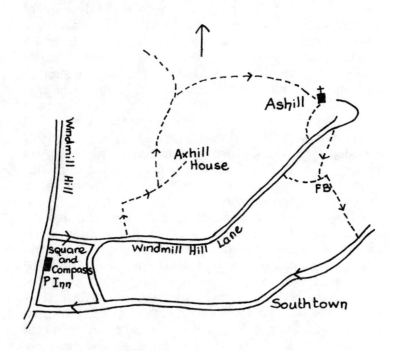

Babcary, *The Red Lion*

There's an extensive menu available at this pleasant old thatched inn, which Mr Pickford told me dates back to the 14th century. Plan your walk to take place at the end of the week, as no food is served on Mondays, Tuesdays or at Wednesday lunchtime. The bar menu includes the normal fare as well as some unusual items - sausage sizzle and Cumberland ring being particularly popular with the regular customers. Draught Bass is the real ale available.

Free House   Owners: David and Diana Pickford
Tel: (045 822) 3230   O/S Ref: ST 5628

Parking: Mr Pickford has no objection to people using his car park, providing that they patronise his inn.

Your walk will take about an hour and a half; it lies partly along quiet, narrow, paved lanes and in the middle section follows the track used by drovers when

taking stock to market. Turn right from the car park, and make for the church. If for no other reason than that Parson Woodforde (of *Diary of a Country Parson* fame) was the curate here in 1764-5, it is worth calling in. The church dates from the 14th century, and is built of local stone with tiling from Ham Hill. There is some fine stone carving within, and if you look carefully at the outer gates of the porch, you will see wood taken from the rood screen when it was demolished at the time of the Reformation.

When you leave the church, continue along Babcary Lane, past Garston Bridge and past the Old Rectory (a big house on your right). You'll see a grassy lane leading off to the right, take that and when it reaches the 'T-junction', turn right: this is Wastover Lane. Ignore the left turn and follow the path along until it joins a track at a ford. If the ford is flooded, as it was when I did the walk, go through the gate into the field on the left, and skirt the field to the little foot bridge and then turn left into Ham's Lane. Otherwise, go across the ford, and turn left, still keeping to a grassy track (Ham's Lane). Eventually you'll come to rising ground with a view across the fields to Glastonbury Tor, just beyond a house called The Withies. Turn right when you reach the road, ignoring the left turn and you'll soon regain The Red Lion Inn, with its cosy bar and welcome refreshments.

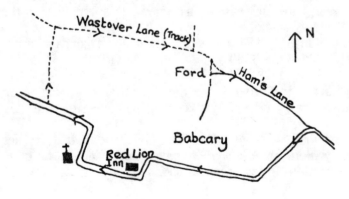

Bridgwater, *Great Escape*

This modern pub, situated on Clare Street, near the Angel Development, has been open for about nine years; the decor is 1930s, and the interior is spacious, with plenty of room for dining. Because of its central location, and the fact that fewer people frequent the town at night, meal catering in the evening is limited to functions. Lunches are served daily, and when I visited, every table was occupied. The food is good, the menu is extensive, offering a wide choice of popular dishes, ranging from the usual bar snacks, salads, burgers, sandwiches, ploughmans, jacket potatoes with various fillings, cottage pie, to barbecued chicken, sirloin and rump steak, with a choice of desserts to follow. Every day the chef prepares two specials (roast loin of pork or braised steak with vegetables when I went there), and I found the vegetables to be especially well cooked and presented.

Various beers are stocked, but only one real ale, Wiltshire Special Bitter from Gibbs Mew of Salisbury, was available.

Free House   Licensee: Steve Nolan
Tel: (0278) 428125   O/S Ref: ST 3037

Bridgwater, situated astride the River Parrett with its extremes of tide, has more to offer the visitor than first appears. The name derives from the 'Bridge of Walter' - a reference to Walter of Douai, who came to this country with William the Conqueror, and who presumably built the wooden bridge that appears on the town's coat of arms. A castle once dominated the water front; built at the time of King John, nothing of it remains now apart from the water gate with a stretch of the curtain wall beyond.

The time to visit Bridgwater (if you can arrange it) is undoubtedly the nearest Thursday to November 5, Guy Fawkes Night. Tourists come from the Continent for the Carnival, which some say is the finest in Britain - others claim it is the best in Europe. Enthusiasts band together in clubs to build magnificent floats costing hundreds, sometimes thousands, of pounds. Floats 40ft high and 100ft long are the norm, all lit by thousands of light bulbs, and towed by a tractor or a lorry, suitably disguised. Up to 120,000 spectators have lined the route in recent years for a procession that takes more than two hours to pass, and the money raised is distributed to various charities.

Parking: when you enter the town, follow the parking signs to the long-stay park on Mount Street, opposite the new shopping development at Angel Place.

Your walk will take about an hour and a half, provided you don't stay too long in the Museum. Turn left out of the car park into Mount Street past the Magistrates' Court and Police Station. Follow the road round to the left and on the right, across from Bridge Enterprises, is the remains of the Glass Cone, a stack that once rose 120ft, dominating the surrounding buildings. It was built in 1720 by the Duke of Chandos as a glassworks. By 1729 it had become a pottery with three small kilns inside for making pots, tiles and sanitary pipes. When demolished in 1942, the cone provided 1,500 tons of hardcore for airfield runways at Ilton and Westonzoyland. Further along on the left, an anchor set in cobbles is a reminder of when Bridgwater was a thriving port. Beyond is the Admirals Landing public house, and the former Ware's warehouse, once used to store bonded goods and grain and since converted to flats. The docks are now a marina. Across the bascule bridge are early 19th century Russell Place Cottages. Retrace your steps over the bridge, noting the ancient stone steps leading down to the dock basin to your left; turn right and follow the path beside the river. On the opposite bank is what remains of the brick and tile works, upon which much of Bridgwater's 19th century prosperity depended. In the industry's heyday roofing tiles, along with Bath brick (a forerunner of Ajax), were exported.

Pass Valetta Place - the building on the corner was once a basket-maker's shop; cross the pedestrians-only Telescopic Bridge (now an Ancient Monument), then turn right and re-cross the river by the adjacent bridge. Take care here, the traffic can be heavy - and fast. Turn left along the bank of the river; you'll come to The Lions House, which now houses the Citizen's Advice Bureau. Considered by Pevsner to be the best house in town, it was built in 1720 of local bricks by Benjamin Holloway for his own occupation. Holloway was a carpenter and builder employed by the Duke of Chandos, and it was probably he who built the houses on Castle Street (reckoned to be the best street in town) between 1721 and 1723. A few yards beyond The Lions House is the Water Gate Hotel, which was built onto the East Gate of the castle - you can get some idea of the thickness of the walls by walking a few feet into the opening beside the hotel.

Resuming the walk, turn right and continue beside the river to the Public Library, founded by Carnegie in 1905, and now the headquarters of Somerset County Council's Library Service. Blake Gardens surrounding the Library are worth walking through. Exit onto Dampiet Street and turn left at Blake Street. Here is the Admiral Blake Museum, housed in the famous man's birthplace. The Museum is open from 11am to 4pm throughout the year, Tuesday through to Saturday. Unlike many places with free admission, this one really is worth visiting, and the volunteers who staff it are knowledgeable about Bridgwater's history.

Leave the Museum and turn left out of Blake Street, pass the Unitarian Church where Coleridge preached in 1797 and 1798 (although he was briefly a soldier and, so far as I can discover, was never ordained, his father was a clergyman). Turn right at the Rose & Crown. Where Marycourt Shopping Mall now is (left side of the road), is where Judge Jeffreys is said to have watched the hanging of Bridgwater's rebels of 1685, following the Monmouth Rebellion. Nearby is the Baptist Church, first built in 1692 behind a row of old cottages (later demolished) and rebuilt in 1837. Beyond, the Old Vicarage, now a restaurant, is one of the three medieval buildings in Bridgwater to have survived the fires that have devastated the town (the others are St Mary's Church and Blake House). You'll see an exposed section of wattle in the wall at the entrance to the car park.

St Mary's Church was closed when I visited, but if you wish to see it, call there before noon.

Walk through the covered market, go right along the High Street (here traditional 'squibbing' takes place after the Carnival), alongside York Buildings.Then go into King's Square where the town's war memorial stands in the central gardens. Keep to the right and walk down Castle Street where each house has a different portico, but so designed to make a harmonious whole. The Art Centre, housed in a house on the right was the first such centre in England after the war. Return to the top of the street and take the lane on your right to Chandos Street. Turn left (this brings you to the other side of King's Square) and then right, bringing you to the Police Station and the car park.

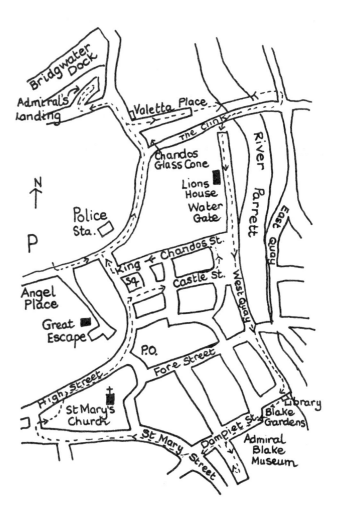

Bruton, *Blue Ball*

Where the inn now stands was previously the White Hart, which was where the gentry stayed in the 16th century, being the best place in town. In 1731 a disastrous fire occurred and by 1765-1770 things were bad enough to warrant the place being sold and parts rebuilt as the Blue Ball Hotel (presumably the fire plate in the Forge Bar comes from the earlier building).

The food here is simple and well cooked, and the service pleasant. The blackboard menu offers dishes such as fried chicken, fish and scampi, all served with peas and chips, along with the usual bar snacks of sandwiches and jacket potatoes ('run of the mill, but varied', according to Jane Hopkins). I found that my child companion was received kindly, and she was delighted with the fish and chip meal tailored to her 3-year-old size. Wednesdays seem to be a favourite day for walkers and, as the pub is gaining a reputation with such folk,overnight guests are offered drying facilities.

Two real ales are stocked, not always from the same brewery, and as the clientele are mainly local people, they obviously approve of having a change.

Free House   Proprietors: Brian and Jane Hopkins
Tel: (0749) 812315   O/S Ref: ST 6834

Parking: Although the streets are fairly narrow, parking is not the problem you'd expect. There's a one way system of traffic control, and you'll find that you'll be led across the bridge near the church and if you bear right onto Silver Street, there's a small park on the right near the Packhorse Bridge, or further up the hill (Plox) you'll find a layby marked by broken white lines opposite King's School (founded in 1517). If you visit during school holidays, or at the weekend, you're unlikely to have any difficulty.

Your walk will take not much more than an hour and leads mostly along quaint alleys and narrow back lanes, uphill and alongside the river. Make first for the High Street, which is across the river via Packhorse Bridge, alias Bruton Bow, and up the hill through the nearest alley (called a barton). Turn left, have a coffee at the Coffee House; ask for a free copy of the Chamber of Commerce's *Discovering Bruton.* Turn left out of the arcade and cross the road. You might be tempted to explore the first turning right, and St Catherine's Hill, but go a few yards more and look across the road at Sexey's Hospital (you can't see it easily close to). Founded in 1619 by Hugh Sexey, a former stableboy who rose to become auditor to Elizabeth I and James I, this former almshouse is occupied by elderly people. If you can, visit the 17th century Hall and Chapel.

Near the bottom of the hill, turn right into Mill Dam. There you'll see a wonderful collection of ornamental waterfowl. My favourites were some splendidly white ducks with powder puffs on their heads.Continue along the path until you reach the lane and turn right; go up the hill – here the map seems to be at slight variance with the lane markings – you'll be on Tolbury Lane and, where it meets St Catherine's Hill, go straight across to Higher Backway. Look for the white wooden gates on the right, with their attractive ornamentation. The walk leads you past the County Primary School (left) and the town Museum on your right. At the end of the backway, turn right onto Coombe Street, cross over the High Street and go down Patwell Street with the Pump on the left by the river. Cross the bridge, and go up the steps into the churchyard. On the wall is a marker, reckoned to be short by 3ft, showing where the floods reached in 1917, causing extensive damage in the town; a flood relief scheme initiated in 1984 ensures that such damage no longer occurs.

St Mary's Church has two towers, the smaller dating from the 14th century, and the other, at the west end, from 1449. Inside, the chancel was rebuilt completely in 1743 to a design by Nathaniel Ireson, an architect and builder who lived at Wincanton. Its blue and white plaster reredos makes that part of St Mary's vaguely reminiscent of a Wren church, while the main body of the building dates from the late 15th century. The nave and chancel are separated by a rood screen, above which is the rood, the crucified Christ attended by Sts Mary and John, erected in 1938. Incidentally, the Royal Arms of Charles II were found in a builder's yard before the 1939 war, and were restored and replaced.

Leave the church and turn left along Silver Street, which leads into Plox (in the 19th century spelt Plocks, meaning small field). On your left is the Rectory, built of stone taken from the Abbey ruins, then incorporated into the buttressed remains of the Abbey wall. The Abbey, although disestablished by Henry VIII, was not pulled down, but was sold to the Berkeley family, and in 1621 and 1644 Charles I stayed there. It was demolished in 1786.

On the right is the cobbled approach to Packhorse

Bridge and just beyond that is the Old House, belonging to King's School, parts of which date back to the original foundation. Past the Abbey wall, look left up the hill to the 'dovecote' whose purpose has yet to be determined. Carry on up Plox and down to the junction with the road called Lusty. Cross Leggs Bridge (built first in the 1550s but now mundane enough to bear heavy traffic), and follow the path to the right into High Street. Opposite Mill Dam is Mill Lane, to your right. Go down here, past the little houses opening onto the lane, and turn left along Lower Backway. Looking up at the backs of the buildings on High Street, with their gardens sweeping down toward the river, I had the feeling of stepping back four hundred years, with little interference from the time in between. Take the first or second barton to the High Street to find your lunch. Return to the car via Patwell Street, over Church Bridge, turn right into Silver Street and along Plox.

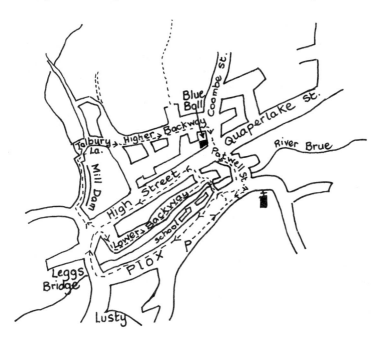

Cannington, *Kings Head Inn*

This inn, situated in the middle of Cannington near the Post Office, is crowded daily. The attached restaurant dates from 1642, but the King's Head itself goes back to the mid 19th century. At the back of the building is a beer garden set in a traditional cottage garden, and this is popular for families in summer.

The lengthy menu is listed on a blackboard above the door to the bar, and includes the usual fare such as breaded fish, quiches, jacket potatoes, omelettes, etc, as well as two special dishes of the day. The evening meal is more elaborate, featuring, among other starters, prawns in various guises, followed by several chicken main courses, along with steak or gammon.

The real ales on tap are Boddington's and Flowers IPA.

The pub has recently received an award for excellence from the Guild of Master Caterers by recommendation of its customers. The licensee, who with his wife has been 17 years in the trade, was born only three doors away, so knows the district well, and can answer guests queries. En suite accommodation is available.

Free House   Licensee: M.Andison
Tel: (0278) 652293   O/S Ref: ST 2539

Parking: is limited at the pub, but street parking away
from the main road is available in the village.

**This is a walk for fine, slightly breezy weather, not for
a hot summer day. It will take 2½ hours and leads
across farmland and alongside the River Parrett.** Begin
by heading along the main road toward Bridgwater, and
turn down the 'dead end' street past some old cottages.
Keeping to the left path, pass through a gate beside the
Equestrian Centre, and follow the track through the
golf course. The path turns right at a farm building and
should follow straight along the field boundary, but if
the planned waymarking has not yet been done, follow
the wide track across the cattle grid and keep to the left
of the field boundary and you'll reach the bank of the
river more quickly; both routes are marked on the map.

If your knowledge of the Parrett is limited to the
narrow stream at Bridgwater, this walk will be an eye
opener. Once past the Agricultural College land, the
gates that mark the field boundaries on the river bank
become less easy to negotiate, and you'll have to climb
at least three. The path leaves the bank and passes over
rough pasture for one field, then after regaining the
bank you'll walk past two more fields, the second far
wider than the first; an electricity pylon on the opposite
bank is a good marker. Negotiate the gate and strike
inland, keeping to the right hand side of the hedge.
This brings you to a ruined stone building at the corner
of the field. The track is easily discerned, but can be
really muddy once you've reached Hallick's Farm, a
trim house with a triangle of grass in front. Keep right
and when broken bricks begin to appear in the path
you'll have reached what remains of Waldron's Farm.

Soon after this the track becomes metalled and then

27

you'll begin to pass housing. Not far past 'Harp View'
look to the right for a footpath. This leads over fields
back to Cannington, and the church is in direct view
almost all the way. Exit onto the main road opposite a
telephone box, turn right, and you'll soon reach the
King's Head.

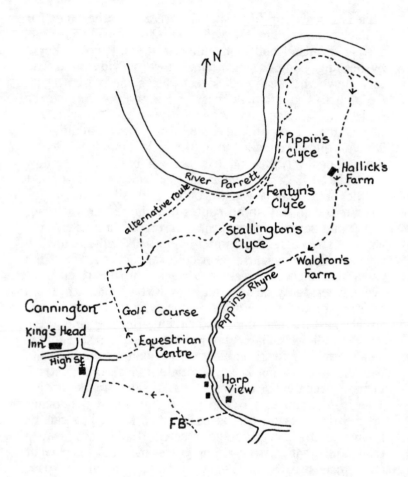

Doulting, *Abbey Barn Inn*

This handsome old stone building fronts a fork on the road leading from Shepton Mallet to Frome. Built in 1725 it is listed and is named for the Tithe Barn that still stands about 50 yards along the minor road. The food is home cooked and ranges between sandwiches (at a very reasonable price), jacket potatoes and the usual bar snacks, to 16oz steaks for the hearty eater. Real ales are on tap including the locally brewed Butcombe 6x. Bed and breakfast is available, and for evening entertainment there's a skittle alley.

Free House   Licensee: A.H. Warner
Tel: (0749) 880321   O/S Ref: ST 6443

Parking: there is no car park at the inn, but the minor road at the fork is wide enough to allow for parking.

Your walk will take just over an hour and leads across fields on rolling hillsides and around a small wood. If the weather has been wet, wear waterproof boots. Begin by crossing the road from the inn and taking the path toward the church, turn right at the first of the two 'no exit' lanes and follow the path along. It skirts a disused quarry on the right, and then the track enters a little wood, keep to the right hand path, and exit onto a narrow lane down a couple of steps. Turn left along the lane for a few yards, and just beyond the boundary of the wood, you'll come to a stile leading into a field. Take this path, which leads up and over a hill, and continue down into the valley. Here you'll come to the source of the River Sheppey, which runs out of the ground into a stone trough known as St Aldhelms Well. It was here that pilgrims are believed to have washed themselves when visiting the church where the saint died. Take the footpath that leads up the hill and exit at the stile beside the little stone building in the corner of the field. Turn left along the main road and ahead of you is the Abbey Barn Inn.

If you are interested in churches, St Aldhelms is worth a visit for the carved angels in the roof on the north and south aisles, and the architecture is unusual in that the spire is centrally placed.

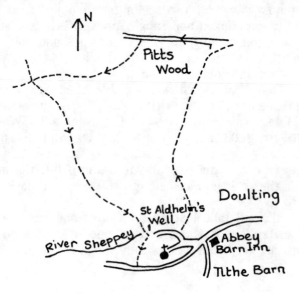

Dowlish Wake, *New Inn*

The pub at Dowlish Wake is somewhat tucked away and
you'll find it, if you follow the signs for Cudworth, at
the southern edge of the village. The inn is by no
means new, dating, so the landlord told me, back to the
time of Elizabeth I; it no longer offers overnight
accommodation so the word 'inn' is a misnomer. The
food makes it worthwhile to visit the establishment. I
chose a most reasonably priced soft herring roes on
toast for my lunchtime snack – the first time I
remember seeing such an item on a bar menu – and
there were other rarely seen dishes on offer, such as
duck and lamb pie, or the New Inn special omelette,
which I might have tried had I not been filled by the
generous portion. The chef specialises in continental
cooking; if you decide you'd prefer to take your walk in
the late afternoon so that you can savour an evening
meal, try to book a table well in advance, as others,
including Egon Ronay and compilers of *The Good Pub*

Guide have discovered how good the food is. Various guest bitters are served (Otter was on tap the day I called in), along with Butcombe Bitter and Wadworth's 6X; Perry's cider, made nearby, is available.

The New Inn is open for food from 12-1.30pm and 7-9.30pm daily, Monday to Saturday, and on Sunday by reservation only. In fine weather there's a play area in the garden for children.

Free House   Proprietor: David Smith
Tel: (0460) 5241   O/S ST 3712

Parking: the landlord is happy to allow you to use the car park provided that you patronise his inn.

Your walk will take about an hour and a half and leads across fields on rolling country most of the way. Turn right out of the car park and take the first alley to the left. Left again and follow the footpath to the playing field on your right. Cross the field and go over the ditch at about halfway along the boundary opposite (this part of the walk was not clearly defined). Keep going straight ahead to the corner of the field where blue plastic has been placed over the barbed wire to protect clothing as one crossed into the next field. Turn right, skirt the field and go through the opening. You'll see a path to your left crossing the field in a diagonal direction. Go alongside the next field down to the brook (watch out for nettles), cross the bridge, turn left up the hill, or right alongside the stream, as the fancy takes you. Skirt the field to the top of the hill diagonally opposite. This leads to a gate above the sewage works (more nettles here). Take the track and, where it swings left, you'll see a path ahead leading across one field and through a gap into a second. Follow the path to the church.

The church is worth going inside, especially if you're interested in the history of African exploration, as the funeral of John Hanning Speke, joint discoverer of the

source of the Nile, was held here with Dr David Living-
stone as one of the mourners. The Union Jack that used
to fly at Jinja (near where Speke first saw the Nile) was
handed over by the Ugandan High Commissioner at a
service in the church in October 1963 after the country
gained its independence. Also in the Speke chapel is an
early Norman font from West Dowlish church (destroyed before 1700); the graveyard of that church is
still used for the occasional burial.

Leave the church by the path that leads to the village
street and near the gate you'll see, on the right side, a
gravestone commemorating Ludwig Pettersen, pioneer
of the Klondyke, 1898, who was born in Norway, at
Bergen in 1869, and died at Taunton on May 22 1934.
There are no Pettersens in the Taunton phone book and
it would be interesting to know why Ludwig came to
this part of the world, and something of his history.

Walk through the village with its lovely stone cottages and attractive gardens, and on the right is Perry's
Cider, should you be interested in taking home a
memento of your visit. The second left fork is signposted to Cudmore, and a few yards along that road is
your lunch.

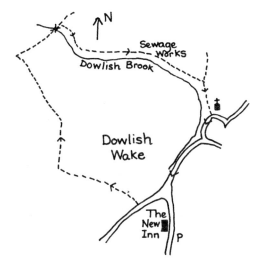

Dulverton, *The Lion Hotel*

This 18th century coaching inn offers year-round overnight accommodation; all bedrooms (1 family, 4 double, 4 twin and 4 single) have en suite services.

The restaurant and bars are popular with local people as well as with tourists, many of whom come from overseas, as Dulverton is an ideal centre for visiting Exmoor. Only two real ales are available, Ushers Best Bitter and locally-brewed Exmoor, but I'm told the beer is good. The food is excellent; home-cooked, mostly using locally-grown produce and featuring two special main courses daily, followed by the chef's Sticky Toffee Pudding, made to an original recipe and to be avoided by dieters (but if you follow the walk, you'll be able to justify taking those extra calories on board).

Free House   Licensees: J. and D. Mackinnon
Tel: (0398) 23444   O/S Ref: SS 9127

Parking: the Lion's parking facilities are limited, but there is a car park one block away behind the hotel and although you'll have to pay, the charges are not high. If that park is full, there is another nearer the river (follow signs to the National Park Information Centre).

This is a muddy and steep walk, so be warned: wear stout shoes and if you have a walking stick, carry it. From the bridge, the walk will take about 1½hours and leads uphill through wooded country, then returns down a steep descent. Cross the bridge and turn right. The walk follows along and above the River Barle, and as the track climbs the hill, you'll have some beautiful views of the surrounding countryside. The path is well signposted (follow the 'Trail' marks), leading through Burridge Wood, an SSSI (Site of Special Scientific Interest), so designated because of the plants that grow there. Burridge is mostly ancient woodland but sadly the invasive rhododendron has gained a roothold, and once established is difficult to clear. This plant, attractive while in bloom, has such a dense growing habit that other plants cannot compete, resulting in the creatures that rely on native vegetation losing their food supply and having to go elsewhere.

The stone cairn on the left soon after the start of the walk commemorates Miss Abbott of Dulverton and Mr Herbert of Pixton who enabled the NPA (National Parks Authority) to buy the wood at a token price. If you look across the valley and up the hill to your right when you get higher up, you may be able to catch a glimpse of Pixton, a large cream coloured house among trees just below the summit of the hill.

At the second 'dip' of the trail the path divides; ahead is an old ford, but the trail turns left, over privately owned land for about a quarter of a mile, and it's along here that you're most likely to see the slot marks of deer.

At the top of the hill (and going up here you'll be glad of that stick) pause to catch breath and take a look at the next vista. You've nearly reached the summit and soon the path will lead downhill – where the mud and need of that stick *really* begin! On the way across the top of the hill look out for Oldberry Castle, thought to be an Iron Age fort.

After negotiating the steep track down the hill, you may need to clean your footwear – across the bridge there's a concreted slope, built to help the ducks get down to the Barle, but useful access to the water for muddy humans. Go up through the town and enjoy your lunch; if your car is in the top park, I suggest you take the road opposite to the one you followed down to the bridge (Dulverton's two main streets are built around a triangular central block). The church, if you are interested, is at the top of the town, beyond the Lion, but I was too hungry to call in.

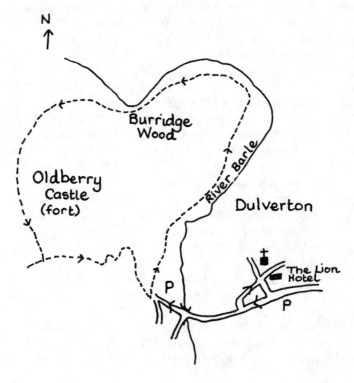

Frome, *The Three Swans*

Documentation for this pleasant little pub goes back to 1749, when it was an ale house and leather shop. The ambience is inviting, the food well cooked, generous in portion, and the place is well patronised. Apart from a menu giving the usual items such as sandwiches, bar snacks, salads and main courses, several boards list special meals of the day, including two (roast beef, vegetables and dessert; steak and kidney pie and dessert on the day of my visit) offering a discount for Old Age Pensioners, and another expressly for vegetarians.

Two real ales are on tap, Ushers Best and Founders. Should you wish to stay overnight, bed and breakfast accommodation is available in one single and two double rooms.

Free House   Licensees: Alan and Mary Snowdon
Tel: (0373) 464768   O/S Ref: ST 7747

Frome is a delightful old town that began as a mission settlement founded by St Aldhelm about 685. In the

Middle Ages it prospered and became an important centre for cloth weaving. The Napoleonic Wars that heralded the decline of the woollen industry and brought starvation to many another West Country town did not affect Frome so badly, as the area already had a diversity of industry, including a bell foundry, established in 1680 in Bell Lane. Later came a printing works and, in 1855 a local clockmaker, J.W.Singer, set up a brass and iron foundry. This foundry became known nationally when it cast the statue of Queen Boadicea that stands on the Embankment at Westminster. Much of the old town survives (although developers in the 1950s and 1960s managed to knock down buildings that should have been preserved); happily, conservationists discovered 17th century industrial housing in the Trinity section of town in time to stay the developers' hands, and much of the centre has been declared a Conservation Area of National Importance.

Parking: drive down the hill into the town centre from whichever direction you come, and leave your car in the park off Cork Street (National Westminster Bank on the corner), near the Public Library.

Your walk will take just over an hour (more if you go into some of the public buildings) and covers much of old Frome, going up and down several steep hills. Bring your camera; this town is most photogenic. Make first for the little (modern) wooden bridge that links the shopping precinct and the library; it crosses the River Frome, and if you look north you'll see the backs of the shops that line The Bridge, which was built in 1667 and is contemporary with Bath's Pulteney Bridge. Few people realise as they drive through Frome's main street that they are crossing a river. It's interesting to think that at one time Frome was considered more important than Bath.

Leave the car park by the Pay Meters and go straight

38

across the road to the lane marked Public Footpath. This takes you up a hill. On the left you'll see a large building, the United Reformed Church, turn left into Whittox Lane and slip through the second entrance gate to the church grounds (opposite No.10, built 1693); go round to the right and you'll see a tiny building that looks a bit like a lock-up - this was built in the 19th century as a Sunday School, presumably to prevent the noise of children disturbing their parents at worship.

At the top of the lane, turn right into Catherine Street, and then left into High Street at The Sun; we tend to think of High Streets as having shops, but this is a residential area. Take a left turn at Wine Street, and then left again into Sheppard's Barton, which was built early in the 18th century to house weavers. Turn right onto Catherine Hill, and keep right where the road divides, with the path rising above the roadway at Maidments; this takes you into Paul Street, which then becomes Palmer Street. Turn right into Bath Street and pass the elegant shell of the old Methodist Chapel at the corner of Rook Lane, on your right; it's a fine example of an early non-conformist church, and was once a source of civic pride.

Cross the road, bear left at The Lamb, and left again into Gentle Street, a cobbled passage. On your way down the hill, you'll pass a private house on the right called Waggon and Horses; once an inn, the stage coach for London used to leave from its yard. The lane goes back to the very early days of Frome - St Aldhelm is said to have walked this way; in medieval days it was known as Hunger Lane, and then later it was renamed for a local family. At the bottom of the lane is St John the Baptist Church; if you like visiting churches, you'll need to arrive before 1pm while it is still open. Carry on past the church a short way and look to the right at the very unusual Via Crucis (Way of the Cross) in the church grounds; the carving of the figures is magnificent. Retrace your footsteps beyond the entrance and go along the path that bisects the graveyard; at the bottom you'll see the Auction Rooms. Viewing days are Mondays and Tuesdays, sales take place on Wednesdays. Turn left down the hill and left again at the Fish & Chip Shop (street unnamed). Note the well on the left at the corner of the churchyard wall – in May this is dressed with a floral picture. Just down from here you'll see the sign of the Three Swans where the food is good.

Cross to Cheap Street, with its central leet to carry the stream from the well down the hill, and glance at some of the shops. Turn right near the bottom into Apple Lane and look up Apple Alley to see just how closely houses were built in the days when people walked everywhere and there was no need to allow width for the passage of vehicles (if you venture up the alley, be careful, the paving cobbles are very uneven and haven't been kept in repair like the ones on Cheap Street.

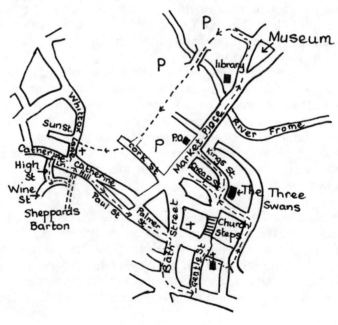

Turn right into Market Place, cross the road at the traffic lights near the Blue Boar. You'll see an imposing-looking building on the right, beside the river. This is The Blue House, a Grade I listed building dating from 1726, when it was an almshouse and school for boys; now it is occupied by senior citizens. A bit further along, on the left, is the Frome Museum, housed in the Frome Literary & Scientific Institute and staffed by volunteers. It's open from 10am until 4pm from Wednesday to Saturday, and is well worth a visit. Opposite the museum on fork leading left, is the Black Swan Guild's craftshops, art gallery and restaurant – you're welcomed warmly when you go in and there's much of interest to see. Turn left into Justice Lane after leaving the Guild shops and you'll come to the Library and the car park.

Glastonbury, *Who'd A Thought It*

In the 18th century this Grade II listed place was a farmhouse and outbuildings. A reminder of that time is in the well (glassed over) over which customers walk upon entry. Accommodation is available in seven en suite bedrooms. Food is served every day and although it sounds simple and humdrum, house specialities are the cheese, pickles and fruit ploughmans, and home-made Irish soda bread. A table d'hote menu is available. Children are welcome and are catered for.

The bar has a nostalgic theme with 30's music. The beers on tap are: Blackdown Porter, Hardy Country, Palmers Traditional and Draught Bass; Eldridge Pope Keg Bitter is also available.

Free House   Proprietors: Liz and Bill Knight
Tel: (0458) 831039   O/S Ref: ST 4938

Glastonbury is like no other town in Britain; variously associated with the birth of Christianity in England, with pop festivals, ley lines, the occult and the healing power of crystals, you'll find here year-round plenty to interest you, even if you just sit on a wall outside St John the Baptist's Church to watch the passersby. The ruined Abbey was founded in the 7th century, and is supposed to have been built on the site of a chapel that Joseph of Arimathea, himself a tin trader and uncle of Jesus Christ, founded. But as there is no evidence of the story until several hundred years after the Crucifixion, the legend is more likely to have been created as a means to encourage pilgrims when Abbey funds were low. Arthur and Guinevere are claimed to have been buried before the Sapphire Altar in the Abbey, but the evidence rests on a report that at the time of Henry II the tomb was excavated to reveal the bones of a tall man and a woman whose long golden hair crumbled to dust as the air entered. Myth or fact, there's something special about Glastonbury, as I hope you'll agree.

Parking: is no problem; so many people visit the town throughout the year that ample provision has been made for cars. I used the park off Northload Street, in front of which is the Who'd A Thought It pub.

Your walk through the streets and alleys will take about 1½ hours if you don't visit the Abbey. From the car park turn right to the Market Cross and go up the High Street to St John's Church. Opposite the entrance is the former main gate into the Abbey Church, later used to house the Guildhall and now some interesting shops. Near the path in the churchyard is a thorn tree, struck from a piece of the Glastonbury Thorn said to have grown from Joseph of Arimathea's staff when he pushed it into the ground on Wearyall Hill. The church has a beautifully carved stone pulpit and a most unusual niche in the chancel. The tomb of John Alleyne in the north transept, dated about 1500, is said by some to be that of Joseph of Arimathea because of the initials JA, but there's no foundation for the story. You'll see several legends illustrated in the East window and in the window near John Alleyne's tomb.

When you leave the church take the path to the west into Norbins Road (North Binne=north enclosure); take the second turning right onto St Edmunds Road, and turn right again onto a path running between houses, which will bring you back to the High Street via a car park. Almost opposite diagonally left is a lane containing a row of 19th century cottages. This opens into Silver Street, at the foot of which is a (closed) gate giving entry to the Abbey grounds. Until the beginning of this century there was a porter's lodge on this site.

Turn left up Silver Street, and right at the top into Lambrook Street. At the High Street end there was once a large pool where livestock was watered and carts washed. It was filled in after a local scold was ducked and nearly drowned there by the local people. To your right is the wall of the Abbey grounds, and Lambrook gives way to Chilkwell (Chalice Well) Street at Dod (dirty) Lane. If you wish to visit the Chalice Well continue to the left along Wellhouse Lane and you'll see the sign on the left for the well. Here is the site of another legend associated with Joseph, for he is said to have buried the Holy Grail here, the cup used by Christ at the Last Supper, and in which Joseph caught some of His blood at the Crucifixion. The waters are slightly coloured with the blood still (so 'they' say).

Turn right onto Bere Lane and call in at the Rural Life Museum, housed in the Abbot's Barn. Here an interesting collection of old implements is arranged to show how the land was tilled in bygone days. Keep to the left side of the road and make your way down to the town via Magdalene Street. Not far from the roundabout is Magdalene Close, and through a little archway to the left is St Margaret's chapel and to the right is what remains of the old almshouses, now converted to old people's flats.

Leaving St Margaret's, continue until you reach the zebra crossing (traffic can be heavy and too fast coming into the town), and if you haven't been there before, call in to look at Glastonbury Abbey. You'll find plenty of literature about the ruins, and some of it is free with your entry fee, so I won't describe them.

Recross the road, continue towards the Market Cross and turn left onto Northload Street and your lunch.

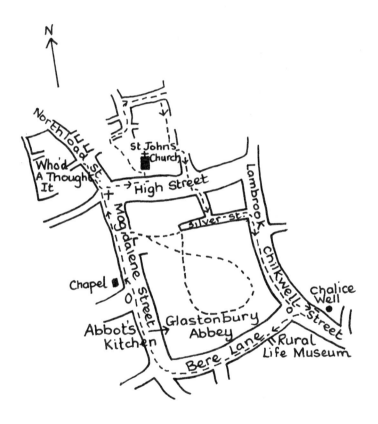

Holford, *The Plough*

Tourists flock to this 16th-century inn in the summer months (accommodation, while no longer available at the pub itself, can be arranged by the landlord), and during the winter locals pack the bars at weekends. The building is beside the A39 Bridgwater/Minehead road, and so is easy to find.

Bass and Exmoor Ale, along with guest beers are on tap. The food is plentiful and home cooked, with a wide variety that includes sautéed venison and poached salmon, with a special menu at weekends. The kitchen is open for orders from noon until 2pm and from 6.30pm until 9.30 throughout the week (7pm on Sundays). The special dishes change with each day and the chef offers charcoal grilled meals in the evening.

Free House   Proprietor: R. White
 Tel: (0278) 741232   O/S Ref: ST 1541

Parking: is no problem; there's a large park across the

lane from the rear of the pub, and a smaller one at the front. The landlord has no objection to walkers using the park, provided they are going to patronise his premises - and by the way, well-behaved children are welcome, and dogs are allowed in the bars.

Your walk will take about 1½ hours and leads along quiet footpaths beside a stream and then goes up onto one of the Quantock Hills with marvellous view over the surrounding countryside. Follow the road that runs between the front of the Plough and the service station. You'll pass the little church of St Mary on the left. Buried in the churchyard is Frederick Norton, composer of *Chu Chin Chow*, the first musical that could be described as a 'hit'.

I took this walk in early May when the streams were running fast with water draining off the hills, and when leaves were newly opened on the trees and the air was full of birdsong, and if you do the same, you'll hear the sound of running water for most of your walk.

Keep following the road to Combe House Hotel - the metalled surface gives way to an earth path. The hotel once housed the tannery that gave employment to local people. A large water-wheel beside the hotel drove the machinery, and after the tanyard closed in 1900 and the buildings were converted, the wheel then powered a dynamo to supply electricity for the hotel and nearby cottages, as well as driving the stone cracker in the quarry and various industrial machinery.

Past the hotel and up the track you'll come to an open area (to which some people drive their cars and then walk). Ford the stream, begin to climb the hill, but ignore the path to the right that leads straight up the hill. Keep left until the track divides, then cross over the small stream, and continue to ascend, keeping to the left. The stream peters out, but the path is clear. Up here you'll see lots of blueberries (whortleberries) and bracken - the latter is spreading and is a problem for those who manage the Quantocks because, like rhododendron, it takes over from native plants, and also is poisonous to livestock. Sheep roam these hills, as do deer, though you'll only be likely to spot the latter at dawn or dusk.

Near the top of the hill where four paths meet, turn right, and continue for a short distance to the crest of the hill. And what a vista awaits you – the coastal plain spread out below, with Bridgwater Bay beyond, and slightly to your right, the landmark of Hinckley Point (Nuclear) Power Station, a modern intrusion on an ancient landscape, but one that provides employment for many people and power for many more.

Almost to the bottom of the hill, take a left path; not as wide as the one you were on, but well defined. It backtracks down to a stream where it joins a wide path.

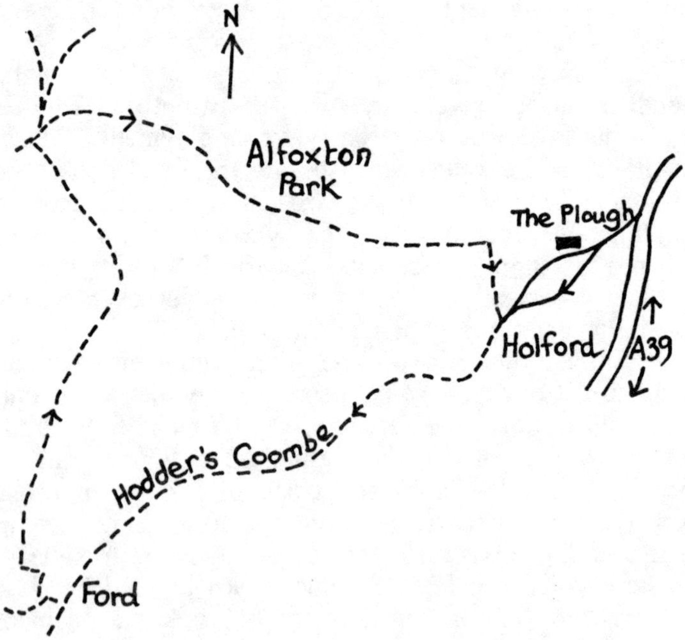

N

Alfoxton Park

The Plough

Holford / A39

Hodder's Coombe

Ford

In this area some walkers have left the main track and made short cuts for themselves, resulting in erosion of a fragile soil covering. Please try to keep to established paths. Turn right at the stream and you'll emerge at Holford Village Green. Turn left along the road to the Dog Pound where stray livestock once were held. Continue up the road towards Alfoxton, where William and Dorothy Wordsworth spent a year to be near their friend Coleridge, who lived at Nether Stowey. At the public footpath sign on the right, go down the hill to the bridge, cross the stream, emerge onto the road, and turn left. On the way back to the Plough you'll pass The Dye House, which is near the site of dye pits used by the silk factory that was established in Holford Glen by Huguenots in the 16th century and which collapsed in the late 18th century. Enjoy your lunch.

Knapp, *Rising Sun*

It's worth taking this walk for several reasons – two of them concern this pub. Firstly, it's probably the best example of a 15th century Somerset longhouse that one may visit without having to ask the owner's permission, and secondly (and more importantly), the food here is excellent, and while there are reasonably priced bar snacks, such as 'meal in a baguette' with various fillings, including minute steak or smoked salmon, if you enjoy superbly prepared fish, then push the boat out and come prepared to spend more on a memorable dish. It's almost unnecessary, with the success of the Real Ale campaign, to record that three real ales are on tap – Bass, Exmoor and Boddington's.

The pub (no overnight guests, so it isn't really an inn but Tony has a list of b&b establishments) is off the beaten track and such is its reputation that the place is crowded to the doors at weekends. If your party has more than two persons, it's better to phone ahead and book a table.

Free House   Licensees: Tony and Wendy Atkinson
 Tel: (0823) 490436   O/S Ref: ST 3025

Parking: is no problem – pull into the pub car park, tell the landlord you're taking a walk and will be back in just over an hour.

Your walk will take about an hour; the first section leads across fields that overlook the Somerset Levels, and the return journey follows a quiet lane back to the pub. Begin by turning right outside the car park and going a few yards down the road until you see a stile on the right. For most of the way the Council has done a good job of marking the stiles and the footpath clearly, but there are a few hiccups in the middle. So follow the direction of the arrows as you cross fields and make for the next stile. As you climb up the gently rising ground you'll see more and more of the Somer set Levels to your left (a third reason for this walk), and when the priory-like outlines of North Curry Church are ahead of you, expect the next two or three stiles to be unmarked. You'll cross a little stream with a surprisingly firm plank bridge and, going up the hill, will soon come to a fence stile with a painted arrow confirming that you're on the right path. Keep right and exit onto the road via a stile above a footpath. Keep walking in the same direction for a few yards and then cross the road to take the footpath to the church (between a garden wall and a field). I went there in early April; one side of the churchyard was carpeted with a misty blue, which turned out to be a naturalised sweep of *Anemone nemorosa,* called by some 'wind-flowers'. Inside the church has some attractive stained glass, and is unusual in its architecture in that the walls are of brick, and the windows high up. The local music society was having a final rehearsal for a concert that

51

night, so I didn't stay long. Exit via the path from the main (South) door, and wander through the village.

There are some delightful cottages in North Curry, those near the church are clustered around a fenced green with a War Memorial in its centre. Keep left and have a look at the recently restored Memorial commemorating Queen Victoria's Diamond Jubilee, then turn right, past the Post Office and take the turning beside it. If the shop is open, call in at Pavement Workshop, a small craft shop that has regular exhibitions of paintings and other works of art. Just beyond there to the left is Knapp Lane.

The way back to The Rising Sun is on metalled road from now on, so if you prefer to walk on fields all the way, go straight on and pick up the path where you first came into North Curry. I wanted to make a circular tour and, as traffic is very light in the area, I went along Knapp Lane, and at the T-junction turned right, beside Peppercorn Cottage. At the fork, keep right, and you'll soon reach another fork; keep right, and at the bottom of the slope is The Rising Sun - and take a moment to examine the inn sign, it is truly unique - the landlord as a Japanese soldier standing under the Rising Sun flag.

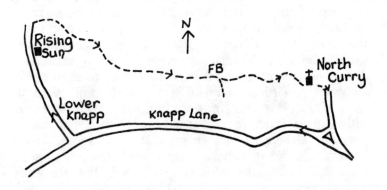

Mells, *The Talbot Inn*

This inn dates from about 1470, with 17th and 18th century additions, and is built of Doulting ashlar, with stone tiled roofs. There are several bars; the one to the left as you enter through the archway is open only in the evening, but beyond that is the main entrance porch and your refreshment. Bass, Butcombe, Wadworth's 6X and a guest ale are all served straight from the cask, and there's an extensive menu of home cooked food available. In fine weather families with young children generally prefer to use the tables in the courtyard but, provided they are well-behaved, children are always welcome. Overnight accommodation can be arranged; book well in advance as this is a popular area for visitors.

Free House   Proprietor: G.F. Crompton
Tel: (0373) 812254   O/S Ref: ST 7349

Parking: the landlord of The Talbot Inn is happy to

permit parking in the inn car park provided you'll be returning for a meal, and that you ask permission first. The park is east of the inn, beyond a small service station.

Your walk will take about an hour and is especially recommended for a hot day as it follows alongside the Mells Stream for much of the way. Go east past the inn, past the lane leading to the church (we'll come back to that later), and pause briefly when you reach the beautifully simple War Memorial on your left. It was designed by Sir Edwin Lutyens and, unlike the majority of memorials at that time, the names of those who died are listed in strict alphabetical order, with no mention of rank, status or regiment. Thus the bright stars of the two wealthy families, the Asquiths and the Horners, are recorded among all the others whose loss brought equal heartbreak to humbler homes.

Keep going east until you reach the crossroads and take the road signposted for Great Elm. You'll pass two cottages on the right and not far beyond them is a gateway with a well-defined path leading alongside the river. Turn right onto the path, which is quite straightforward, and will need no further instructions until you reach the paved road. For a short distance all you'll see will be trees and flowers, but soon you'll notice on the left side that under the dense vegetation there's a wall of cut stone, and then the walls become increasingly high, and some of them are of brick. Then you'll see derelict buildings among the vegetation and you'll have reached the heart of an industrial complex that brought prosperity to the people of Mells, Great Elm and Nunney. In the 19th century skilled craftsmen produced agricultural tools that were exported throughout the world, and which were so well made that examples are still in use today.

This complex was developed by the Fussell family in 1744 when James Fussell took a 99-year lease on land belonging to John Horner, the local landowner. At first Fussell bought up old iron and reworked it, but by the beginning of the 19th century nine waterwheels, powered by a natural fall that had been harnessed into a weir (still there), were operating forges, hammers and grindstones. Two branches of the business were in operation, belonging to different members of the family. The Upper Works made shovels, spades, billhooks, axes and breast ploughs; the Lower Works produced scythes, reaphooks and hayknives. Between the two factories was a 'ropewalk' where straw was twisted to be wrapped around the edged tools. Such was the companies' pride in the quality of their tools that all were stamped with the special mark accorded to each craftsman so that any faults could be traced to the maker.

Steam power gradually replaced the water power, and then, to 'improve' upon the old-fashioned hand-forging that had made the firms so successful, rolling mills were installed at great expense. The process took many years to perfect and by the time the technique had been mastered the business was in decline.

Isaac Nash of Bellbroughton in Worcestershire made an offer for the works in 1894 and, in an early example of asset stripping, auctioned off everything he could and left the buildings to decay along with the men upon whose work the Fussell's wealth had grown. There's a slightly eerie feeling about walking through the complex, but it's also most fascinating – I don't recommend that you search them out, but there's a network of culverts running under the site, the main one of which is 165 yards long.

Shortly after leaving the site you'll come to clipped grass and gardens on the bank above the river, and soon you'll join the road. If you prefer to keep to footpaths, retrace your steps, but if you want to make a round trip, turn left onto the paved surface and follow it back to Mells.

Call in at the church and see the memorial to Edward Horner, the last male heir to the estate, who was killed at Cambrai in 1917. The memorial consists of a horse and rider cast in bronze, and was the first equestrian sculpture by Sir Alfred Munnings, the famous painter of horses. The base of the statue was designed by Lutyens and is a scale model of the Cenotaph in Whitehall. Also in the church are some beautifully worked kneelers, all different.

In the churchyard lie the remains of several well-known people including Lady Violet Bonham Carter and Ronald Knox, the Roman Catholic theologian.

Turn right at the foot of the lane leading from the church and you'll be back at The Talbot Inn.

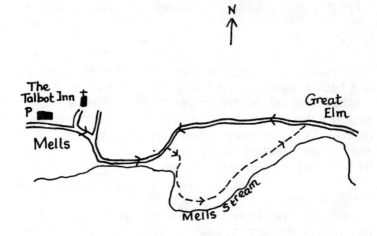

Middlezoy, *The George Inn*

This brick and stone pub was built in 1624 as an inn and has remained so ever since. Until fairly recently a smithy operated at the rear of the building but the premises have now been absorbed into the kitchen of the George. The place had a moment of notoriety in 1947 when the then landlady, aged 73, was murdered by a Polish serviceman. The present licensee, Sue Kirk, was 2 days old at the time, and was born in the house opposite the inn.

Although away from the main road, it's worth visiting the George if you're a real ale enthusiast – it has held the title of Real Ale Pub of the Year for the Southwest Region, and hopes to gain it again. Real ales include John Smith, Tawny and Harrier (both from the local Cotleigh Brewery) and a guest ale. The food menu is not ambitious, but contains interesting items such as plaice with mushrooms and prawns in a wine sauce, garlic chicken in a wine sauce, a vegetarian nut paella, along with the usual dishes with chips and a variety of sandwiches and burgers and salads. There is also a daily special available, and Sunday lunches are a feature of the cuisine. The desserts are made by a lady in the village who specialises in the kind that cause slimmers to add another week to their diet regime just with the one meal. Prices are moderate because Sue Kirk believes customers should be able to eat here often rather than for the occasional treat. There are two pleasant unspoilt public rooms, a lounge and the public bar – and it's a joy to go somewhere with no intrusive piped music. The local clientele are welcoming, and you may well find yourself staying on beyond the time planned. But not to worry, if you feel like staying overnight the inn offers bed and breakfast accommodation.

Free House   Licensee: Sue Kirk
Tel: (0823) 698215   O/S Ref: ST 3733

Parking: there's a large car park behind the George, and you're welcome to leave your vehicle there while you go for the walk.

Your walk will take about 1½ hours and leads mainly across fields and along drove roads above the Somerset Levels – Middlezoy stands on a slight rise in the middle of the wetlands, and if there has been rain in recent days, you'll be wise to wear boots or waterproof shoes. Turn left out of the car park and just past the Post Office, go left over some steps, walk either side of the wall and continue left down the lane (Back Lane). Ahead is a drove road; after about 800 yards, go right over a gate (it's often overgrown around here) and then half left across two fields. A stile lies ahead, over a bridge. Go diagonally across the wheatfield (the farmer does not like walkers skirting the edge) to the stile that leads into a cider apple orchard. Turn left and follow the track straight ahead until you reach a stile on the right, cross the field, go through a narrow alleyway until you reach a big slate slab, step over it, continue past the church, then bear right to reach the main road and turn right. Keep along the main road until you reach the narrow lane at the corner of the cemetery; turn left and follow along it back to Middlezoy. It has little traffic and eventually you'll reach some bungalows. Turn right here and you'll soon see the pub.

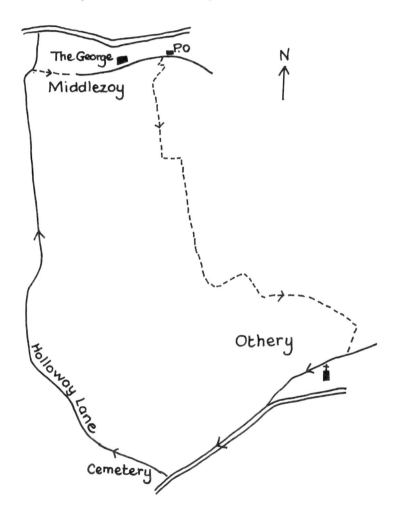

Milverton, *The Globe*

The 400-year old Globe is one of two surviving pubs in the village where, in the last century, there were four as well as two beer retailers. It was built as a coaching house with stables underneath (it's on a hill). During the middle years of the 19th century, it is believed that one of the upper rooms was used as a meeting place for worship by Wesleyan Methodists. The inn offers accommodation but none of the three bedrooms is en suite.

The pub is unpretentious; John Smith's and Ushers only are on tap, but both the beer and the cider are good. Although the menu is not extensive, the food is home cooked and reasonably priced, including such items as beef casserole and cottage pie along with the usual bar snacks and chicken, fish and steak main courses. Food is available throughout the week at lunch time and in the evening, apart from Sunday evenings.

Courage House   Licensee:Brian Jenkin
Tel: (0823) 400534   O/S Ref: ST 1225

Parking: the Globe has space for at most five cars on the pavement outside, so you'll need to park in the free car park at Creedwell Orchard, just a few yards further on into the village.

Your walk will take about 1½ hours and after beginning on village streets will follow footpaths over fields that are inclined to be muddy. Turn left out of the car park and go down the hill to the Health Centre, keep going alongside some lock up garages and if you stay on the left side you'll be able to see more easily the backs of the old buildings that face onto Fore Street. The path passes through Jubilee Garden, Milverton's little hidden 'park'; on the right you'll see the remains of what was considered a holy well, hence the name of the lane, Thornwell; it emerges into Fore Street. Turn left, and at the top of the street, turn right up the hill. Halfway up is High Street; unlike most High Streets this one has no shops and no exit. Beyond the houses on the right take the footpath to Wood Street. Turn left; at the bend in the road is a footpath beside the house called The Mount, this can sometimes be muddy, but there's a far muddier place further along, so it's wise to wear sturdy shoes or boots. A stile at the top of the path leads into a field; keep left and, where the footpath signs point both right and left, take the left path through the gate. A well-defined path leads across the field down to another gate, and it's here than you'll encounter a great deal of mud (I had three attempts at this walk). A second gate to the right is difficult to lift but it is waymarked. Keep left to regain High Street.

At the end, cross the road to St Michael's Church. It dates back to Saxon times, with a minute portion of the original building incorporated in the Lady Chapel. The north face of the tower still carries traces of markings for the game of Fives. The cedar trees mark the burial pits of victims of an outbreak of a plague in the 17th century. Inside the church, the medieval bench ends are reckoned to be among the finest in Somerset.

Leave the church by the path that skirts the grave-yard on the east side and go into Parsonage Lane. Turn left. The house on the right was formerly the Parsonage and was built mainly in 1480. For many years it was the country residence of the archdeacons of Taunton. At the bottom of Parsonage Lane is the church hall, St Michael's Rooms, built at the beginning of this century to a design influenced by the Arts & Crafts Movement. It's on the corner of North Street, a row of houses, many of them of Tudor origin, but with Georgian façades. You'll return to them soon, but cross the road to Mill Lane and follow it downhill. You'll hear the sound of traffic on the bypass, but this lane is closed off. The mill ground corn from Saxon times until well into this century; some machinery remains, and near the bridge is a wall with pigeon holes in which the birds that fed off the corn lying around nested. The squabs and adult birds were useful when meat was scarce.

Retrace your steps then turn left along North Street. On the left, on the house called Quaker Lodge, a plaque commemorates the birthplace of Dr Thomas Young, developer of the wave theory of light and co-translator in the late 18th century of the Rosetta Stone, the key to deciphering Egyptian hieroglyphics. Continue down North Street, and at the bottom turn right, and you'll soon come to the Globe and your meal.

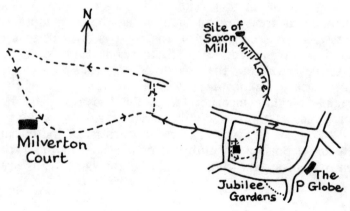

Minehead, *The Old Ship Aground*

This attractively designed pub gets crowded in summer, located as it is at the edge of the quay. There are three bars, with a counter for food in the lounge bar. The menu lists the usual bar type snacks and, appropriately crab and smoked mackerel are offered. Pub meals are available, both at lunchtime and in the evening, seven days a week. Two real ales are on tap, Courage Best and Ruddles County.

It is possible to book overnight accommodation here, but none of the four rooms is en suite.

Courage House   Licensees: Anthony and Susan Phillips
Tel: (0643) 702087   O/S Ref: SS 9746

Minehead has depended on the sea for its existence from the time of William the Conqueror. Early in the 15th century the manor of Minehead was sold to the Luttrells, one of whose descendants gave Dunster Castle to the National Trust in 1976, 600 years after the family first bought it. In 1616 George Luttrell spent

£5,000 to build a stone harbour at Minehead to alleviate the problems of the natural harbour silting up. With this new amenity the port developed from a fishing hamlet, with the occasional cargo vessel putting in to unload, to being a prosperous sea-going centre. Sailing ships set out for the New World, the West Indies and Mediterranean ports from here, and coastal trading vessels offloaded coal, wool and other commodities and took on West Country goods. Trade declined during the 18th century and was just beginning to recover when, in 1791, a fire broke out in the yard of a mill at the foot of Bampton Street and spread through the town. Some 70 dwellings were destroyed, rendering homeless between 400 and 500 people. Several warehouses and store rooms were also destroyed, and with them the livelihood of many families. Little rebuilding was done until the 1820s, as the Napoleonic Wars also served to depress the economy.

Improvement in road surfaces and the establishment of a regular coach service in the 1830s led to Minehead becoming popular as a holiday resort for the more affluent early in Victoria's reign. The building of the railway in 1874 brought greater numbers of holiday makers and led to a boom in the hotel and boarding house trade. Today people still flock to the resort, but many make for Somerwest World (formerly Butlin's Holiday Camp), and so many former boarding houses are now private homes.

Parking: drive to Minehead via the A39 and, at the roundabout at the entrance to the town, follow the left-hand fork (Townsend Road). At the end, Wellington Square, turn right again, then half left into Blenheim Road, and left again, following the signs to the car park up the hill (Martlet Road).

Your walk will take about an hour and after a stroll through the town, will take you alongside the sea and

then up onto the hill with wonderful views to the Welsh coast. From the car park a signposted foot-path leads down into Market House Lane; if you turn left and follow the lane to the bend, you'll see the stump of the Market Cross, which was where, in the 16th century, a regular market was held. The almshouses on the left side were built in 1630 by Robert Quirke, a local merchant, as eleven separate dwellings for distressed, impotent (?), poor persons. Elderly people still live in the houses, but the places would not be recognisable to their earlier inhabitants, having been modernised in the 1980s after an anonymous donation was helped by funds from the local council. Look up at the curfew bell above end house nearest the cross stump – said to have come from one of Quirke's ships, it was rung each morning at 6am to remind men to begin work.

Turn left at the end of the lane into The Parade, and walk to Blenheim Road, crossing to the right side and into Blenheim Gardens. Continue alongside the sea and pass the Promenade Hotel into Quay Street. This was where fishermen and harbour workers lived, and at one time there were houses on the seaward side, making for an exceedingly narrow lane, but a storm that caused considerable flooding led to their demolition in about 1910. A photograph dated 1900, in the town's archives, shows the Red Lion Hotel (on your left) as a thatched and whitewashed building. Just beyond there is Church Path – if you're short of time, turn up there, otherwise continue along Quay Street to look at the cottages. The cottage called The Old Customs House superseded another customs house located by the Quay. By the 18th century silting of the harbour had caused the larger vessels to dock at Bridgwater, Bristol or Watchet, so the town could no longer afford the expense of a regular customs officer and smugglers moved in. A report states that a Quay Street house was recently found to contain a small concealed cavity with a block and tackle left behind by a smuggler.

There are several interesting harbourside buildings: the old Pier Hotel has been refurbished and now called the Old Ship Aground is where you are recommended to have lunch.Look around the Lifeboat House and imagine how it must have been in 1901 when it was first built and the lifeboat was propelled by oars. By the harbour is the chapel of St-Peter-on-the-Quay, which began life as two cellars or warehouses erected by Robert Quirke; their rent paid for the upkeep of the almshouses. One cellar was demolished late in the last century and in 1910 the other was rebuilt and consecrated as a fishermen's chapel. The nave slopes downwards so that the altar is below street level.

Leave the chapel, retrace your steps to Church Path, and climb to Weirfield Road. Turn left to St Michael's Road and continue past the War Memorial to the church. Go in, if only to see the great treasure of the church, Richard Fitzjames'Missal, a handwritten service book dating from the late 15th century, and reckoned to be one of the finest of its kind in the country. When you leave the church, cross the road and go down the Church Steps, stopping to admire the attractive old colour-washed thatched cottages. The tall chimneys were essential to make fires draw in a place where the steepness of the hill and the crowded houses served to restrict air movement. At the bottom turn left into Church Street, then right to Middle Street. The houses on the left were built as a workhouse to replace one at the foot of Church Steps. Go left along Watery Lane, past the school. At the end turn left into Park Street.

Cross the road to Wellington Square to look at the statue of Queen Anne, a gift to the people of Minehead in 1719 from their former MP. Swedish-born Jacob Bancks was an ardent admirer of the queen and when he saw her effigy set up at the West Front of St Paul's Cathedral in London, he so admired it that he commissioned the artist Francis Bird to carve the second white alabaster statue. Bancks represented the town from 1698 to 1714, despite some protests (from others who wanted the position) that a foreigner shouldn't be allowed to be an MP. Perhaps the fact that his wife had been the widow of a Luttrell helped to overcome the obstacle?

Having admired the statue, walk down the Parade to the sea front and retrace your steps to the Old Ship Aground.

North Newton, *The Harvest Moon*

Food is served in this pleasant modern (30-year-old) pub daily, except Monday, from noon until 2pm and 7 to 10pm. Among the bar snacks on offer are sausage and apple burgers, and leek and ham rolls, which are fresh leeks rolled in smoked ham covered with cheese sauce and served with French bread. The main dish menu includes lamb and apricot pie, an interesting-sounding change from the ubiquitous steak and chips.

As Devenish has no brewery, the beers come from Whitbreads, and the real ales on tap are Castle Eden, Flowers Original and Flowers IPA.

Devenish   Licensees: Sue and Tony Hughes
Tel: (0278) 662570   O/S Ref: ST 2931

Parking: is no problem. Leave your car in the yard of the pub (opposite the village school).

Your walk, which follows mainly alongside the river will

take nearly an hour. right out of the car park and visit St Peter's Church, built on Saxon foundations. The two ladies who were polishing the pews when I called in told me the parish celebrated its 700th anniversary in 1992. The building is low and wide, with a fine Jacobean carved pulpit and rood screen, and an unusual East window. The Alfred Jewel, now deposited in Oxford's Ashmolean Museum, was found near here, and a replica hangs on the wall just inside the entrance. When you leave the church, turn left out of the churchyard, follow the little lane past the mill and cross the Bridgwater-Taunton Canal. Turn right and take the towpath, noting on the left the pillbox, now hidden by vegetation, and built to protect the village during World War II. At the next bridge turn right and follow the road past Coxhill Farm. At the junction, go right, still keeping to the road until you reach the green Public Footpath sign on the left. This leads into what looks like a set-aside area, with a recently established copse of broad-leafed trees, and emerges onto Tuckerton Lane. Turn right, and then right again opposite Steps Farm. Follow the brook that fronts the new houses and leads back to the village. Turn right for the last time, and ahead of you is the Harvest Moon and refreshment.

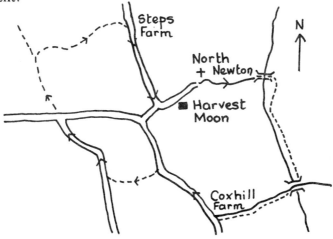

Porlock Weir, *Ship Inn*

The picturesque thatched 16th century Ship Inn and adjoining 19th century Anchor Hotel operate as a centre for yachtsmen and walkers as well as for those who want to spend time doing nothing but watch others being energetic. The Ship has two bars and if you've ever regretted the demise of the public bar, sigh no more, there's one here. The lunchtime menu consists mainly of snack-type food; it's well presented and enjoyable (I had crab and lettuce sandwich - with brown bread) The evening menu looked inviting; the chef's speciality is steak and kidney pie made to a traditional recipe, and aficionados come time and again for it. The real ales available are Exmoor and Ushers, both local brews.

There's plenty of accommodation here for overnight guests; the place is highly recommended by Egon Ronay and Ashley Courtenay, so make early reservations.
Free House Proprietors:Pandy Sechiari & Donald Wade
Tel: (0643) 862753   O/S Ref: SS 8747

Parking: a large municipal car park is opposite the inn and costs £1 for stays of up to five hours' duration (two hours at 50p doesn't allow for a leisurely lunch).

Your walk will take about 1½ hours and partly follows the route established by smugglers as they carried contraband cargo landed away from the eyes of the customs men at Minehead. It's well defined and has several steep stretches and one really muddy section, so use waterproof footwear if you can. Take the path that runs between the Ship and the Anchor. Behind the Anchor Hotel, lime kilns once produced fertiliser for the moorland farms. As you climb the hill you'll have a good view across the bay; the 'Weir' derives from the name given to rows of stakes driven into the beach to catch salmon that used to run in these waters. The harbour, built in 1422, was famous for its oysters, which were dredged from a bed kept secret from poachers (such was the fame of Porlock oysters that the Colchester boats came to poach, but the men didn't know to look for the whitewashed cottage chimney that served as a landmark for the legitimate oystermen). When oysters weren't in season (no 'r' in the month), they were stored, or 'perched' in shallows opposite the cottage called Oyster Perch and turned every three days.

The path leads over two stiles and through two gates and then goes along the road for a short distance. A bridleway leads off left near Worthy Manor; when you reach the footpath to the right, at Lovelace Cottage, ignore it. Keep to the bridleway, it parallels the road above the stream and is more comfortable for walking, with more gently inclined gradients than the road. Above Yearnor Mill is a bridge and this is where the path from the road joins the bridleway (should you have succumbed to the lure of the 'footpath' notice).

The bridleway divides just before Yearnor Bridge is reached; keep to the left track and where it again branches for Porlock and Porlock Weir, take the latter path. It crosses a bridleway coming up the hill. The occasional red painted flash on trees indicates that you're on the right path, but where the track begins to lead downhill you'll notice several small paths off to the left, and these obviously are where walkers without sturdy footwear have found it necessary to retrace their steps to circumvent the waterwashed and muddy 100 yards or so of pathway encountered where the track swings left.

At the painted red arrow turn left, then right onto the path above Porlock Weir. Zigzag down the hill behind the white houses, turn right when you reach the road and then left back to The Ship Inn and your lunch.

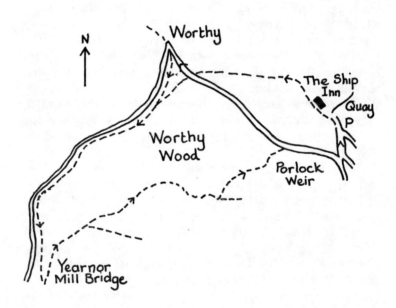

Priddy, *Hunters Lodge Inn*

Hunters' Lodge Inn is large and unpretentious, dating from the end of the 18th century. It has been run by the Dors family since the early 1900s, and although it was once an inn, accommodation is no longer available.

The food offered is basic and excellent, tailored to meet the needs of the clientele who flock to this place – farmers, potholers, cavers and walkers. Despite plenty of picnic tables in the two gardens at the back, and tables in both of the bars, many customers in summer have to eat standing up, and so all food can be eaten using just a fork. From October to May, cottage pie made with maincrop potatoes is on the menu; faggots made by a Wells butcher are a speciality, two pasta dishes, one for vegetarians, and chili con carne are also available. Newly baked white bread accompanies each meal, and the price is such that a family of four can eat for what one main course would cost in many more upmarket places. Barrels line the wall behind the bar counter, containing a choice of three real ales - Bass, Butcome or Oakhill (formerly Beacon Brewery). Farm cider from Wookey is also on tap - and again the price is surprisingly low.

Free House   Proprietor: R.G. Dors
Tel: (0749) 672275   O/S Ref:ST 5250

Parking: is easy; plenty of space beside the pub, and if you should arrive on a particularly busy day, roadside parking stretches for miles.

This walk is best done on a bright, breezy day when you feel like filling your lungs with clean air. It leads across tussocky terrain and along a very muddy drove road, so wear waterproof boots if possible. It will take about two hours, a little more if you want to look more closely at the pond or at the barrows. Cross the road from the pub and go uphill along the West Horrington road until you reach a 'bend in road' sign not far beyond the building on the right at the edge of the forest plantation. Just past the sign turn left at the better defined footpath (another comes first, but you'll miss the Priddy Mineries Reserve notice with all its useful information if you take that). Walk towards the pond, following to the right if your shoes are water-tight, otherwise take the left fork along slightly higher ground to join the path above the pond at Fair Lady Well. The path divides here, continue straight up the hill, with the fence/dry stone wall on your left. The terrain here is covered with gorse and bracken, but once you are over the stile at the top, that gives way to grass. Go past the earthwork and the strange-looking concrete building on the left, through the gate and into the field with the nine barrows - these burial mounds were found to contain Bronze Age articles and are just a few of the prehistoric remains in this part of the county. If you have time, wander over and around the barrows, the reason for their existence has not yet been satisfactorily explained.

Head down the hill toward the cattle troughs in the middle of the boundary of the field and exit over the stile; turn left at Nine Barrow Lane, and immediately turn left again onto a muddy drove road, which leads up and over the hill back to the Wells road. Not far past Eastwater Farm you'll see the green painted hut belonging to the Eastwater Cavers, one of three caving groups in Priddy. The village, besides being the most northerly in Somerset, is also the highest and lies on limestone. Lead has been mined here since prehistoric times, and according to Alan Thomas, in his *Story of Priddy*, conduits from the remains of the Temple built in Jerusalem in 1014BC were analysed at Massachusetts Institute of Technology and concluded to be made from lead mined in the Mendips. Then the Romans came here, probably mainly for the lead to make the pipes that were all-important to their bath-loving culture, and the course of their road and the remains of their fort and a settlement are just below the radio mast that rises in the background beyond the Hunters Lodge to your left. Turn left onto the Wells road and just past the garage, on the right is your destination.

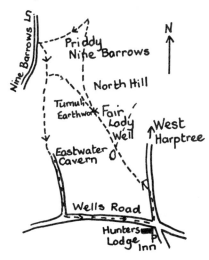

Shepton Mallet, *Butterflies Wine Bar*

This wine bar, housed in one of the truly old buildings in the centre of Shepton Mallet, was previously a wet fish shop. It became a wine bar in 1978 and also serves beer and cider. Over the years it has built a reputation for good, low-priced food. The board menu lists the usual bar snacks of sandwiches, salads, jacket potatoes, ploughman's, etc, along with starters and main courses and each week offers a different two-course special with coffee to follow, costing less than many main courses.

Overnight accommodation is available. The age of the place is evident in the uneven walls and the absence of any right angles, especially in the little restaurant beyond the bar.

Only one real ale is served, Wadsworth's 6X, by popular demand.

Free House   Proprietors: Clive and Janet Cater
Tel: (0749) 4995   O/S Ref: ST 6143

This is a very old town; the Romans came here – the site of pottery kilns lies west of the medieval centre. King William took the manor from the Saxon overlord and gave it to a Norman baron, but otherwise was not interested in the town. The present name comes from an early 12th century landowner surnamed Malet.

Two waves of immigrants in the 14th and 16th centuries, including French Huguenots, brought new skills especially in textiles. Shepton Mallet's prosperity was based on wool; at one time some 30 mills were driven by the power of the River Sheppey, but the end of the Napoleonic Wars and the invention of machinery to increase production led to widespread unemployment, and riots broke out when men became desperate at seeing their families starving.

The wool merchants built handsome homes, some of which survive, but sadly, during the 1950s and early 60s developers stepped in and many historic buildings were torn down. Fortunately, a few old places remain, and for the most part they have to be sought out, but one old building has a high profile, and that's Shepton Mallet Gaol (or Jail), which, built in 1627 at a cost of £320, is the oldest House of Correction still in use in Britain. The masons at that time earned the equivalent of 2p a day, and labourers somewhat less.

Parking: Butterflies has no parking; nearby at Great Ostry is a large municipal car park.

Your walk, which will take about an hour, leads along narrow streets and alleys on a fairly steep hill. Begin at Great Ostry, walk through the narrow passage to exit onto Town Street. Turn left past the market cross and right into Church Lane. Ahead is St Peter & St Paul's Church. It's worth visiting. It contains a magnificently carved stone pulpit dating from about 1550; when first made it would have been painted and must have looked superb. The roof, considered to be one of the finest in the West Country, consists of 350 carved panels, each one different. Near the entrance is a font bowl, relic of the original Saxon church, which was found in some-one's garden where it had been used as a flower pot.

Turn right as you leave the church; to your left is the Rectory, built in 1627 as a grammar school. Carved on the wall is the motto *Disce aut Discede* (Learn or get out).Follow the path, keeping right, and you'll emerge into Leg Square, with its handsome old townhouses. Along the river to the east was a corn mill, with three factories beside Barren Down House (across the river and over to your left) and two more nearby – a great concentration of industry, and small wonder that when the economy collapsed in the early 19th century so many workers were affected.

Turn right uphill and keeping right, follow round the walls of the prison into Gaol Lane and turn right at the end into Frithfield Lane. At the bottom of the lane, turn right and walk past the King's Arms (on the left) to the stone wall and entry opposite Swiss Cottage, to see the narrowness of the stream that powered the mill downhill from you. Continue along the road lined with cottages on the left until you reach a path on the right leading to a bridge over the millstream. Pass the prison entry again and continue left up the hill, past Edengrove House (ahead to the right) and The Hollies until you reach Edengrove Lane.

Turn right, go along the path down some steps, over the river, up more steps and straight uphill, with Barren Down House on the right. The lane is paved and has a wall on both sides, over which you can see some pleasant gardens. If you feel energetic and wish to extend the walk, continue right to the end, go over the stile and turn left along the field boundary to emerge onto the highway beyond the District Hospital. Otherwise, take the lane to the left, which leads into Princes Road, turn left at the highway (B3136), and this will lead straight ahead to Town Street. Several of the old buildings survive; the present Midland Bank on the right was once the George Hotel and Post House. At the Market Cross turn right to look at the Shamble, the sole survivor of two rows of medieval stalls that lined the Market Place until the beginning of this century. Nearby is the modern community centre, presented to the town by the Showerings, who were major employers until recently.

Return to Town Street and almost opposite Church Lane is Butterflies and your lunch.

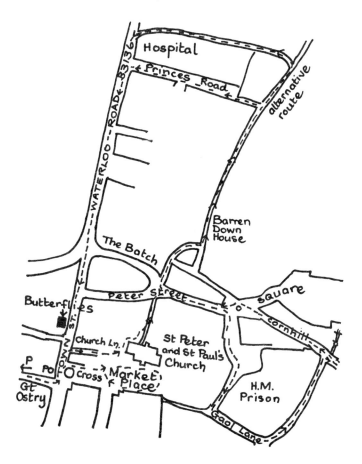

Stoke Sub Hamdon, *Fleur de Lis*

The Fleur de Lis is a 14th century Listed Building that began life as overflow accommodation for the Priory on nearby North Street. The top floor was run by nuns as a hospice, possibly for the tending of lepers. After Henry VIII's Dissolution of the Monasteries, the building became a coaching inn, and although coaches have long ceased to pull up in the yard, accommodation is still offered today.

In the grounds you'll see a 'Fives Wall'. This game, a form of handball, became popular during Elizabeth I's reign and at first was played by ordinary folk using the church wall. In the 17th century bishops objected, on the grounds that the game was damaging church property, and so Fives Walls were built elsewhere, often near inns (The Lethbridge Arms at Bishops Lydeard has another fine example). The game was popular enough to warrant two stadia being built and it has been recorded that £60 was taken in admission money soon after the wall was built. Scoring was done by sticking twigs into holes on a stone slab (rather like a large cribbage board), and what might prove to be the scoreboard was recently unearthed at the house beside the inn.

This pub, being a tied house, serves Eldridge Pope real ales only, but three are on offer. The food menu is extensive and designed to suit all pockets, ranging from soup and a roll, through sandwiches, jacket potatoes and bar snacks via vegetarian fare to a main course of T-bone steak, four vegetables and choice of potatoes. At the weekends and in the height of the tourist season, it would be wiser to book a table.

Eldridge Pope Licensees: Ken and Hilary Yates
Tel: (0935) 822510 O/S Ref: ST 4717

Parking: this can be a problem; the inn has a small car park for the use only of customers, so you'll need to take the Ham Hill road in the centre of the village to reach a) the free car park, or, if that's full, one of the parks actually on the hill.

Your walk begins at the bridlepath to the left partway up the hill from the free car park and will take about an hour and a half. It covers fairly steep hilly ground and also goes through village lanes. Follow the path southwest along the hillside until it reaches the surfaced lane; ignore the footpath signs off to the left, and carry along the lane to the bottom of the hill, then bear right. When you reach the sign for Broadmead, on the right, take to the footpath again, skirting Little Norton, and rejoin the road just at the other side of the village.

Follow the road to Norton sub Hamdon (ignore the left fork to Chiselborough) – there isn't much traffic in that area – and continue along the road until you reach Church Street to the right. Go along that lane to look at the splendidly painted doors at the west end of the church, and also to see the dovecote in the graveyard.

Take the footpath that passes alongside the dovecote,

turn right to eventually join the bridlepath to the left. You'll see Stoke sub Hamdon and its houses ahead, but keep to the bridlepath and continue climbing (good for the leg muscles and heart) – it's a steep climb. Pass through a gate and continue the uphill climb, negotiating a barred piece of fencing at the top. The view from here over the Somerset countryside is worth the effort. From there walk up (or down) the hill to your car and drive to the pub for your meal.

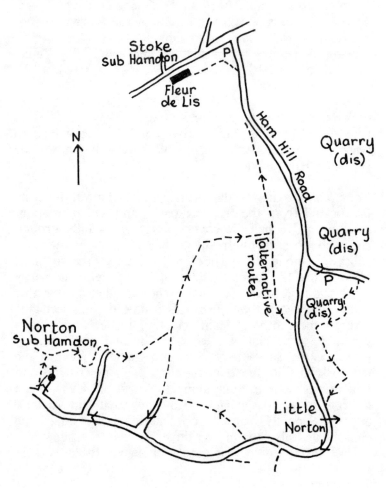

Taunton, *Brewhouse*

I am directing you to this place, which is not a pub at all, but is housed in a theatre, because over the years I have lived in Somerset the standard has remained consistently high, and that cannot be said of many pubs. It has a good bar and an even better restaurant. Staffed by volunteers, it offers exceptional value, and I've yet to be disappointed in a meal I've had there. Also, if you like art, there's usually an exhibition of some kind being staged in the area set aside for refreshment. There's always a choice of hot and cold main courses, a good selection of salads (help yourself) and a tempting array of desserts. Go there if you can before 1pm - Tauntonians know about this place.

Taunton, the county town of Somerset, is mentioned in the *Anglo-Saxon Chronicle* of AD 722; by the time of Domesday it had become a trading centre. In 1129

Bishop William Giffard began building the castle. Later, in 1497, Perkin Warbeck, who managed to convince some people that he was in reality Richard of York and rightful heir to the throne, was at the castle when he learnt that Henry VII's army was only 20 miles away. He fled to Southampton Water but couldn't find a boat, and so petitioned the king for clemency. This was granted, but Warbeck abused the king's trust, and eventually was executed.

At the time of the Civil War Taunton Castle was besieged for a year; Admiral Blake, who held it, received grateful thanks from the Parliamentarians. Apart from the castle, there are few buildings in the town that are really old. There's the Municipal Hall that was a grammar school in the 16th century, and there's the Tudor Tavern, dated 1578, the oldest piece of domestic architecture in Taunton, built as a town house for Lord Portman, and many years later converted to commercial use. Recently the former leper hospital, located on the outskirts of the town and dating to the 13th century, has twice been set on fire by vandals and it has yet to be decided whether restoration will continue.

Parking: there are plenty of car parks in Taunton; some are popular with local people and you'll find them full by 9am; I'd advise you to make for one of several on the north side of the river across from Debenhams. They can be reached by turning east on Bridge Street into either end of Wood Street. Parking is by Pay and Park, so allow at least an hour for your walk – two or three hours if you intend to call in at some of the places of interest on the way – plus another hour for lunch.

Your walk begins at the bridge and is on pavement all the way. Whoever decided to paint the bridge blue and white and to colour the town's coat of arms deserves a pat on the back for lifting the spirits. Walk across towards Debenhams, and turn right along the riverside path. Keep left beyond the paved area and skirt the walls of the castle.

Take the path to the left beside the castle, go through the little gateway, keep left until you reach the entrance to the castle. Call in, noting the wooden framework of the late 15th-century almshouse that has been reconstructed in the forecourt, and visit the Museum.

The main gallery is the Great Hall, dating from the 12th century. Here Judge Jeffreys tried 526 rebels in three days during the Bloody Assizes following the Monmouth Rebellion in 1685 – most of the men were hanged or were transported for life to the West Indies.

Pause as you leave the castle gateway and look to your left at the front of the Castle Hotel – it has one of the oldest, largest and finest wisterias in the country, and in May is a magnificent spectacle, covering the entire facade of the building with pale mauve streamers.

Take the first turning to the right – there's a SWEB shop on the left – and you'll reach a shallow flight of steps leading to Corporation Street. Don't go down to the pavement yet, but turn right in front of the ancient building, erected by Bishop Richard Fox in 1522 for a school, and now used as a Municipal Building. Go in if you wish, and ask to be directed to the part open to the public (a craft show was in the Great Hall the day I went). Turn right again and cross the road. Keep right and, at the the junction of three roads, turn left and stroll for a little way along The Crescent. On your right are the offices of County Hall, to the left are Georgian townhouses, now mainly converted to offices, but at least the facades have been preserved. Retrace your steps to the Dragon Book Shop, the oldest bookshop in Taunton and always well stocked, then take the passage leading beside the shop. This is Bath Place, where horses once paced; now it contains some delightful small shops, including another fine bookshop.

At the end, a 16th century covered way leads to the

pedestrianised High Street. Cross the pavement to the shoe shop on the corner – this was the site of The White Hart, whose landlord in 1848 was Frederick George Manning; a year later, having left Taunton for London, he and his wife became notorious for the brutality of their murder of Patrick O'Connor, a customs officer. Keep going in the same direction away from the High Street and within a few shops you'll come to The Tudor Tavern, with its black and white upper storey and the date 1578 (the coffee's good if you need refreshment). Turn right down the passage just beyond the tavern, and you'll be able to see the Elizabethan exterior of the back of the building. The courtyard leads you into the Old Pig Market (the only pigs to be seen there now are wooden ones, upon which children play and weary shoppers rest). More small shops here and several exits – take the one to the right and you'll come to the High Street again. Turn left, walk to the end, and cross the main road into Vivary Park via the cream painted gates with their coloured coats of arms of the town. Once a part of the Kinglake Estate, Taunton acquired the park in 1895.

The townspeople are justly proud of their parks' department, and the flower beds present a spectacular display throughout the growing season. The park is also home to a collection of ornamental ducks and wildfowl; and, as befits a late 19th century foundation, there's a lovely Victorian wrought iron bandstand surrounded by grass. There's a bowling green and a golf course within the grounds; in 1976 the world non-stop running record was broken in the park by John Barr, who ran 131 miles in 27 hours. For those with less strenuous tastes, the annual flower show is held here in late August.

Leave the park by the main gates, turn right, and immediately right again into Mount Street. Here you will see small Georgian townhouses. On the left are the Jellalabad Barracks; this area, called Tangier, was where

the notorious regiment known as Kirke's Lambs was
billeted during Monmouth's Rebellion, following a tour
of duty in Tangier. The first barracks were built in
1796 when Mount Street was Carpenters Lane, and
were for cavalry. The present buildings, dating from
1878-9, were to house Prince Albert's (Somersetshire)
Light Infantry. Until 1987 the Regimental Pay office
was based here, but now even that has gone. Continue
right round Mount Street, passing on your right the
greenhouses where plants are raised for the town's
floral displays.

Back on Mary Street, turn right, noting to your right
the United Reform Chapel where John·Wesley preached
in the 18th century. Cross the road and take the next
left; it's a dead end road with a pedestrian way beyond.
You'll get to the main shopping centre on East Street
this way. Cross the road and make towards the left,
look for Magdalene Passage (if you reach W.H. Smith's
you've gone too far, retrace your steps), and go down
there. Again, it has some small speciality shops, including a leather shop and a couple of haberdashers.
At the end of the passage turn left. Go into the church.
This is St Mary Magdalene's, Somerset's largest and
most magnificent parish church. The tower is especially
fine; it was built in the mid-19th century to replace one
that was crumbling, and is an exact copy of its prede-
cessor. Much of the building is early 16th century, and
the glory of it (in my opinion anyway) has to be the
roof, with its wonderful gilded angels, more than 200
of them.

Turn right outside the church and walk along Whirli-
gig Lane between old brick garden walls. At the end
you'll come to Middle Street. Walk along until you see
the entry into the Courtyard and go through (more
little shops). Turn right into St James Street, cross the
road and turn left at the mini roundabout where the
road ceases to be one way. This will lead you to your
lunch.

When you leave, cross the car park to the river and make towards the bridge. Cross the road, keep beside the river into Goodland Gardens, and cross the little bridge that goes over the millstream where once the old town mill stood. The bridge over the Tone takes you back to the parking area.

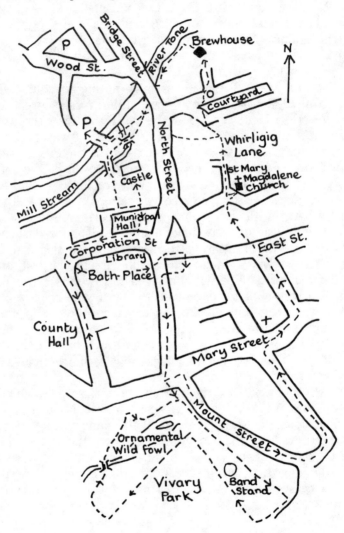

Timberscombe, *The Lion Inn*

The Lion Inn claims to be the oldest licensed inn in Somerset, having received its first licence in 1604. It's still an inn and Mr and Mrs Jenkins have increased the amount of accommodation and have upgraded the public rooms so that there is plenty of comfortable eating space.Upon entering there are restaurants to both sides, and a lounge/family room beside the bar at the back. Courage Directors is the most popular beer; bar meals are available all week from noon until 2pm. The Sunday lunch is especially popular. The proprietor offers a 10% discount on food for parties of six or more ramblers (show her this book).

Free House   Proprietor: Sharon Jenkins
Tel: (0643) 841243   O/S Ref: SS 9542

Parking: is available throughout the village, but you may find difficulty parking on the road when people are at church (I went to the village hall car park).

Your walk takes about an hour, following a track onto the Common overlooking the village, with wonderful views across Exmoor. Follow the road round to the back of the Lion Inn where you'll see Great House Street (No Through Road). Go past Willow Bank up the hill to Holes Square, here the tarred surface goes right; ahead is a track with several cottages on the left. Take that track up the hill until you reach a gate on the right (ahead are two gates and a 'Private' sign). Go through the gate, and at the path division, follow the one to the right marked with red. Go through two gates (this is a well-marked route) and you'll be above the village on the edge of Timberscombe Common. Keep to the right all round the perimeter. When you reach the gate marked with yellow above a line of silver birches, turn left, go down the hill through the tree avenue to a gate also marked with yellow, past metal covered sheds and back to the gate where the markings began. Go left down the track and when you reach Willow Bank, keep left, crossing the stream by the raised path. Take the stone steps past the Methodist Church, and cross to St Petrock's Church. Of special interest is the mural of King David above the south doorway. Leave the church by the front path and the Lion Inn is to your right.

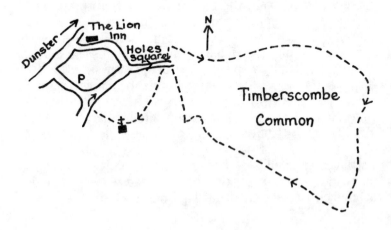

Triscombe, *The Blue Ball Inn*

This delightful thatched inn dates back at least to 1766, when it was mentioned in documents held at the Records Office in Taunton. Always known as the Blue Ball, its first surviving licence is dated 1782. It was built as an inn and posting house because it stood on what was then the main road connecting the ports of Bridgwater and Watchet. Upwards of eight horses were stabled here so that when carts carrying goods for shipment arrived at the inn, additional animals could be slipped into the traces to help haul the carts up the steep hill beyond. At the top the post horses were un-harnessed to make their own way back to their stalls.

Although the Blue Ball no longer caters for overnight guests, the welcome is warm, and the food excellent. Pancakes, both sweet and savoury (including vegetarian fare) are the speciality of the house, and food is available throughout the week from 12 to 2pm and 7 to 9pm; evening meal orders are not available on Sundays.

The Littles are real ale enthusiasts; several are on tap,

including Tetley, Tawny, Exmoor Stag and Burton.
Free House   Proprietor: Mrs A.F.Little
Tel: (098) 48242   O/S Ref: ST 1535

Parking: you may either park in the pub car park, and make your walk a little longer, or you can drive up to the car park near the quarry entrance; at the end of your walk you then drive back down to the pub.I opted to leave my car in the pub park to make it a truly circular route.

Your walk will take about 1½ hours, and leads over high ground. Parts of it can be muddy, and some of the paths are very narrow. Begin your walk at the quarry car park. To the right, opposite the park, a bridle path loops back toward the Blue Ball, climbing ever higher up the hill, so that by the time you are level with the pub, you are looking down on it some distance below. The path swings left and is very easy to follow. It 'kisses' the West Bagborough road briefly, and then goes off to the left. The markings are clear, and after the path crosses a stream and dips downhill, it then turns left and if you're out of condition you'll find yourself stopping frequently to look back across the valley or to look to the private property on your right with its dense grove of rhododendron bushes. Keep climbing, and eventually you'll reach the top of the hill, with a stile to your right. Turn left onto a well defined path; this is part of a network of drove roads (for sheep) that cut across country avoiding rivers and streams as much as possible and keeping for safety to the high ground. Don't be tempted to take the two-track path that forks off the the left, but keep going along the ridge until you see a car park to your left at Triscombe Stone (you'll have passed the cairn that marks Will's Neck, the highest point on the Quantocks at 384m/ 1,260ft slightly above you on the right as you walk along the track). Turn left at the car park, and follow the path downhill, skirting the quarry. Either get back into your car or enjoy the fast downhill pace back to the Blue Ball, and then tuck into one of the savoury pancakes mentioned above.

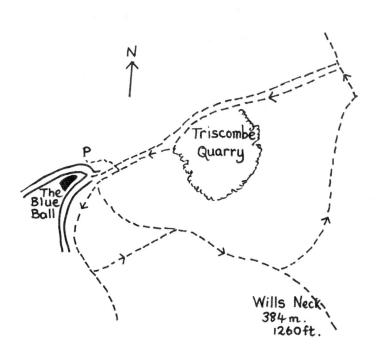

Waterrow, *The Rock Inn*

This 400-year-old inn is one of my favourite pubs; the food is excellent and reasonably priced, the service is cheerful, and the temperature of the beer is just right, possibly because the cellar is carved out of the rock that gives the inn its name, and there's no need for refrigeration, even in summer. This is a real ale house, with traditional ales from two local breweries, Cotleigh and Exmoor. Two local ciders are also on tap.

There is a restaurant for those who wish to have a more substantial meal, but the bar menu is varied, with a choice of sandwiches (the smoked salmon is good), fish dishes, omelettes, home-made meat pies (game, cottage, steak and kidney, and chicken), curries, chili con carne, pizzas, salads, etc; the portions are generous, and most regular customers (and there are a lot) save the restaurant meals for special occasions. Should your visit coincide with a special occasion, you'll have a wide choice, ranging from beef medallions in red wine sauce, duck in orange sauce, pork tenderloin, tornado Rossini, stuffed   plaice with a white wine sauce, all accompanied by nicely cooked vegetables and, for the vegetarian, Stilton and broccoli in cheese sauce with pasta. Sunday lunches are a speciality – a starter (soup or pâté, or sometimes egg mayonnaise) choice between two roast meat courses, with four vegetables, choice of several desserts, followed by coffee (second cup if you wish).

This place is an inn, and if you wish to stay, you'll find the prices reasonable and the rooms comfortable and well equipped. Book well in advance, as the inn is almost always full, even in winter.

Free House   Licensee: B.R.P. Broughall
Tel: (0984) 23293   O/S Ref: ST 0525

Parking: there are two car parks for The Rock; park in the one across the bridge facing the inn.

Your walk is an easy one, going uphill across fields for the first section and downhill along a B road for the final stretch. It will take just under an hour. Follow the side road up the hill – the Hurstone Country Hotel notice shows you're on the right road – and as soon as you   reach two oddly shaped stone pillars, squeeze between them into the field on your right. This is a 'pinch stile', created by local artist Michael Fairfax as part of a new footpath opened by farmer and hotelier John Bone. As you'll be returning to the Rock, you won't cover the entire footpath. Keep to the right, skirting the edge of the field overlooking the river and the copse. If you take this walk in the spring, you'll be rewarded by wild cherry blossom and flowers galore – the fields are managed to encourage the growth of as wide a variety of wild flowers as possible. Pass through the chained stile and keep to the right; go through another chained stile. In the distance you'll see the towering columns that once carried Isambard Kingdom

Brunel's Devon & Somerset Railway (absorbed by Great Western in 1901) 104ft above the River Tone on the Venn Cross Viaduct. Cross the field towards the River Tone, passing the stone trough set in the ground for the use of livestock. Ford the brook and make up the hill to the gate onto the lane. Here, turn right and follow the metalled surface up the hill to the Stawley-Bathealton junction. Turn right and follow the road downhill all the way back to the car park and over the bridge to your lunch.

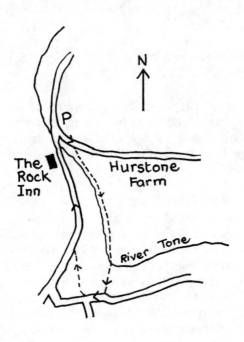

Wells, *The City Arms*

This pink painted stone building served as the city jail for many years. In a document dated 1598 the corporation gave orders to rebuild the jail, and it was in use until 1808. The stocks, gallows and ducking stool were stored in the cellar. For the past 180 years the jail has been a pub.

From the end of October until the end of March, the City Arms is closed between 3 and 5.30pm, but for the rest of the year the place is open all day.

Butcombe Bitter, Ash Vine Challenge and Bass Cask Ale are the real ales on tap. The menu is extensive and contains interesting-looking items, such as mushrooms stuffed with Stilton cheese; smoked chicken and ham salad; smoked trout and prawn salad; ham, avocado and tuna bake, along with more usual offerings. There's a choice for vegetarians, including a stroganoff, a stir fry and a curry dish, a children's menu and, finally, a large blackboard lists the daily specials.

Free House, High Street   Proprietor: Guy Roberts
Tel:(0749) 673916   O/S Ref: ST 5445

Wells is a gem of a city, the kind of place that folk aspire to retire to, almost the smallest cathedral city in Britain (only St David's is smaller). If you can approach either from Bath, or from Bristol, you'll see how the city nestles in the fold of the hills (and the view makes a good photo too).

Wells dates back to the time of Ina, King of the West Saxons, who founded a church here because of the clear waters that bubbled out of the ground, beyond the marshy land of central Somerset, and below the Mendip Hills where outlaws could find cover after attacking defenceless townsfolk. It became a bishopric in 909, but the Normans moved the centre to Bath in 1080 and there it stayed until the 13th century when Jocelin Trotman, a native of Wells, set up his bishop's seat in the present church, which dates from 1180. He conceived the plan for the West Front of the cathedral, but sadly it took 40 more years after his death for the grand design to be completed. Originally the figures were gilded and painted; many were destroyed by the Puritans and others were ravaged by time, but recent work has restored much of the glory.

The springs of water that attracted Ina still flow today, as you'll see when you walk along the High Street. Bishop Thomas Beckington, in the mid–15th century, presented the townspeople with a source of pure water for drinking (the original conduit was replaced in 1799 by the Gothic trough that stands at the entrance to the Market Place), and the overflow kept the street clean in the days before sanitation.

Parking: go to the car park on Princes Road, near St Cuthbert's Church on the Glastonbury side of the town. Unless you stay overnight at an inn that has parking, use a municipal park (traffic wardens abound).

Your walk will take at least 2 hours and will lead through alleys and along narrow street. Begin at the **footpath leading out of the car park:** turn left at St John Street and go to St Cuthbert's Church, the second largest parish church in Somerset. The timbered roof above the nave has been restored to its original 15th century colours. Note the ceiling above the south aisle; this was concealed by plaster until the 1960s when repairs were being carried out and the carved stonework was found underneath. This, too, dates from the 15th century.

Outside the church, keep left along Priest Row; the building adjoining the north side of the churchyard is thought to be unique in England, having a Guildhall on the first floor at the west end, and a chapel at the east, with almshouses in between. The porch was built to bridge a brook, long covered over. Turn right along Chamberlain Street, half left into New Street and across the traffic circle (with care) into The Liberty, whose name pre-dates 1831 when the inhabitants were outside borough jurisdiction. Walk along here, noting the many buildings bearing the little plaque identifying them as belonging to Wells Cathedral School, which celebrated its 750th anniversary in the 1970s. Almost opposite The Cedars is a narrow passage, marked by a guardrail at the edge of the road; go through the passage and call in at the tiny chapel to your right. This is at the top of The Vicars' Close, founded in 1348 to house Vicars Choral and Priest Vicars of the cathedral. The buildings have been in continuous occupation since and the Close is reputedly the finest of its kind in the world. At the opposite end of the close is the gateway that opens onto a bridge leading across to the Chapter

House and stairs of the cathedral. The gateway contains a first floor dining hall, and the treasury. As you emerge from the gateway, turn right and call in at the Wells Museum, once the Chancellor's house and next door to the one-time home of Polydor Vergil, an Italian who became Archdeacon of Wells in the 16th century and who wrote a history of England at the instigation of Henry VII. Later the building housed the Theological College, and is now home of the Music Department of the Cathedral School. With luck you'll hear some most professional sounding practising coming from one of the rooms. The Museum contains a variety of exhibits associated with the area, ranging from lead pigs mined in the Mendips during Romano-British times to plaster casts, made for the 1851 Great Exhibition, of statues on the West Front of the Cathedral.

From the Museum, turn back to the left, walk under the bridge and follow the wall around the Cathedral until you reach the path beside the moat. Apart from the swans, there's a fine collection of various ducks and waterfowl and explanatory boards identify them. If you are interested, parts of the Bishop's Palace are open to the public, otherwise follow the signs to the left leading to the Cathedral. A verger will hand you a leaflet, so I shall not use space to describe the building, but try to time your visit to see the action of the clock. I can recommend the Refectory for a mid-morning snack. After seeing the glories of this most beautiful place, exit across to the left through Penniless Porch, where once beggars solicited alms. Ahead is the Market Place and set in the pavement, to the right, is a brass strip showing the length of Mary Rand's jump when she won a Gold Medal for Britain in the 1964 Tokyo Olympics. Continue around the corner (right) into Sadler Street, where you will follow the line of the city wall, turn left into Chamberlain Street (retracing footsteps for a few yards), and left again into Union Street, a narrow lane with the old Sun Inn on the left. Turn right at the High

Street, and keep going straight and you'll see The City Arms across the road on the left.

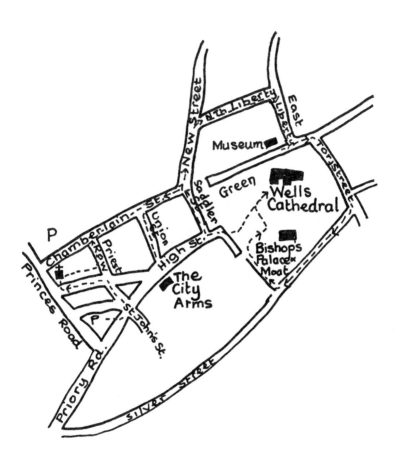

West Bagborough, *Rising Sun Inn*

Built of stone and cob, with a thatched roof, this is a pub that has risen considerably in the world. In the last century it didn't merit a name in *Kelly's Directory*, the landlord being referred to as a beer retailer. The beerhouse was known locally as The Shepherd's Crook; it was sold to Hanbury & Colching, a local brewery, and by 1914 had been renamed The Rising Sun.

Now it is a free house once more, and the pub is an inn that merits Three Crowns rating from the English Tourist Board, and AA listing. Where there once was an upstairs bowling alley are three en suite bedrooms, furnished to a high standard, and downstairs is a fourth room, suitable for disabled guests.

The place is crowded at weekends; on Sundays many locals call in for a pint (and sometimes for lunch) after morning service. Dishes of roast potatoes set at the bar as appetisers are soon emptied, but take care not to blunt your appetite – the fresh vegetables and roast meat that comprise Sunday lunch are served in generous portions and are too good to leave.

During the week the cook offers daily specials, and the menu is worth reading for the wine selections with each dish, along with the interesting comments on the various dishes; some are standard British fare – shepherd's pie, beef stew and dumplings, Lancashire hot pot, but also on offer are starters such as asparagus in lemon and mushroom sauce, salmon mousse, and among the main courses are fish, mushroom and leek pie and kidneys in red wine sauce. I had whitebait and found it excellent. Mozart made a pleasant accompaniment to the meal, and was appreciated also by my fellow diners.

Real ales offered include Boddingtons Bitter, London Pride and Royal Oak, and guest beers. Ken is a wine buff, so a speciality of the house is the choice of wines, 77 in all, many also have half bottles.

Free House   O/S Ref: ST 1633
Tel: 0823 432575 Licensees: Ken, Irene and Ivy Oxley

Parking: is on the side of the road, and can be difficult to find during summer, as the village is popular with visitors. If necessary, continue driving up the hill, turn left at the fork and park at the large car park on Lydeard Hill, and then amend the directions for your walk, taking your meal part way through it – the map will make everything clear, and you'll have the comfort of knowing you've walked off some calories before going home. Make sure you have stout shoes with you.

Your walk will take about an hour if you don't call in at the church. The initial climb is steep, and the track can be muddy. At the top, the trail leads over glorious open land with views across the Quantocks. Take the well-defined track that goes straight up the hill beside the inn. The path is much used by riders, so in dry weather the surface can be rough, and in wet weather, muddy. Several gaps in the hedge to your left afford splendid views across the park of West Bagborough House toward the church, and they give a good excuse to stop and catch your breath. Bagborough House, built about 1730, was owned by the Popham family, one of whose earlier members, as Chief Justice of England, had condemned Guy Fawkes to be executed for his part in the 1605 Gunpowder Plot. The poet William Wordsworth and his wife Mary stayed there in 1841 while revisiting their West Country haunts (they had spent a year at Alfoxton in 1797/8). The stables and outbuildings attached to the Georgian house can easily be seen as you climb the hill. I'm told that in early spring the snowdrops on the lawns are a delightful sight. I walked the path in mid-April when primroses, bluebells, pink campion, herb Robert, celandines and violets made a wild garden of the banks. The church beyond is dedicated to St Pancras, and dates from the 15th century. If you're interested in tombstones, one in the churchyard marking the grave of Eleanor Woodford is worth visiting for the quality of its carved lettering.

But it's time to resume the climb up the hill. Turn right at the top and follow the track that forks to the left to take you further up Lydeard Hill; on a fine day you can see all of Taunton Deane spread below, while across the other way you can see Bridgwater Bay. At the top of the hill, bear right, and follow the track to the large gate beside the car park. Walk over the cattle grid, and down the narrow lane until you reach the wider road at Birches Corner. Turn right, and follow the road down the hill. Above the derelict buildings of Tilbury Farm, to your left you'll see relics of the park attached to the 18th-century Terhill House (long since gone); the first is an enigmatic statue of a man, clad only in a short cloak, gazing out across the hillside. Opinions are divided between him representing the god Jupiter or a huntsman. Together with a folly in the form of a small 'ruined chapel', the statue was most likely put up while Thomas Slocombe (memorial in

Bishops Lydeard church) owned the estate. Further down the hill on the right you'll pass the pretty pink-washed thatched house called Richards Cottage; this has a bread oven projecting outside, a feature that is uncommon in this area, although several cottages at Selworthy and Allerford have such ovens. Entering the village proper you'll come to Higher House on the left, now a successful country house hotel; continuing downhill you'll reach Quantock Pottery, with its wide selection of hand-thrown wares. The pottery is open throughout the weekend and also has a restaurant. The Rising Sun is only a few steps further and the church is just down the hill beyond there.

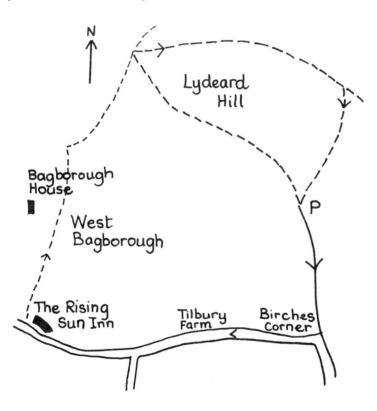

West Coker, *Royal George Inn*

The name of this attractive pub commemorates a vessel that, having been an admiral's flagship at some long-forgotten battle, was present at the Battle of Cape St Vincent in 1780 and then, in August 1782, capsized at Spithead while being heeled over for underwater repairs. Nine hundred men, women and children, died in what was then the worst naval disaster of all time. After that, a lot of inns and public houses were named for the ship.

The pub, which dates from the 18th century, has an extensive menu of home-cooked food, including soups, fish and chips, meat pies served with vegetables, ham, egg and chips, spaghetti dishes, salads and sandwiches served in a pleasant dining area below the main bar. Real ales on offer include Flowers Original, Bass and Boddington. There is no cook's 'speciality' as such, but the presence of regulars on most days (I've visited this place several times) testifies to the quality of the food and the beer.

Free House   Proprietors: Alan & Heather Primmer
                             Alan & Jacky Ivory
Tel: (093) 586 2334   O/S Ref: ST 5113

Parking: there is a large car park behind the George, and walkers are welcome to leave their cars there provided they return to patronise the pub. There are traffic lights almost at the entry and the road (the A30) is narrow at this point, so be cautious when turning in, especially if approaching from Yeovil.

Your walk will take about 1½ hours and, apart from a fairly steep rise at the outset, is easy going all the way, leading along narrow lanes, with the occasional glimpse through the hedge over rolling hills. Avoid this walk during weekdays; part of it follows the road leading to the local tip (tucked well away out of sight) and dustcarts rush past in endless procession.

Turn left at the pub entrance, being careful where the road narrows at the traffic lights – despite the controls, some cars still hurtle along as though their drivers *must* make up extra seconds on the journey. You'll probably have to cross the road to make sure of your safety, but return to the left side when you can and continue along the main road (High Street) until you reach the surfaced path that goes up the hill beside the house called 'Bembridge' (39 & 39A). Climb the hill, with a few stops to look across into the valley. At the top go right along Ridge Lane – rarely used by traffic. Turn right again, then walk along the narrow lane that leads over the A30 until you reach the cross-roads. A third right turn brings you to the Odcombe road, which is the parade route for the garbage lorries.

Just as you near Odcombe, turn right at a little lane and cut through to rejoin Camp Road, which runs along

the crest of the rise. On your right you'll see a footpath sign; cross the field, ignore the lane that you come
to and continue across fields (the stiles are in good
order and the paths are well defined) until at the West
Coker housing estate. You'll cross a small stream and
almost opposite is a path running between the houses.
Where the path divides, turn left and you'll come to the
church of St Martin of Tours. Sadly, access is possible
only on a Sunday, as vandals have forced it to be
locked when unattended. It's an attractive place, dating
back to the 13th century and has an unusual reredos.

Outside the church walk a few yards toward the
village main street and turn left into the path leading
to the Four Acres motel. You'll emerge almost opposite
the Royal George and your lunch.

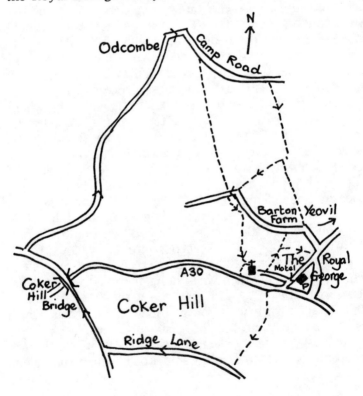

Winsford, *Royal Oak Inn*

This inn typifies the American dream of a British pub – thatched roof, low, timbered ceilings, log fires on large inglenooked hearths – so much so that when the British Exhibition toured New York and other cities, The Royal Oak was chosen as the model for the pub called The Britannia.

Built on the old packhorse route where wool trains would rest after collecting Irish yarn landed Minehead, this inn has experienced West Country history in the making. R.D. Blackmore is said to have written much of *Lorna Doone* here, and Tom Faggis, the highwayman immortalised in the book, lived nearby. Today, the inn, which dates in part back to the 12th century, is more likely to have walkers and tourists sitting in the bars than linen importers or writers.

There's superb accommodation available, should you so desire. In the bars, the real ale on tap is Flowers

Original Bitter and IPA. The food is not expensive, and there's a wide range of home cooked dishes made with local produce on offer. Meat pies, with a variety of fillings, proved to be the most popular on the day I called in, probably because the air was chilly, and people coming in off the hills had developed healthy appetites.Also popular are the seafood platters, which include smoked salmon among the ingredients and home-made pâtés with brandy. Specials of the day are available.
Free House   Licensees: Mr and Mrs C.R. Steven
Tel: (064) 385 455   O/S Ref: SS 9034

Parking: is available at the Royal Oak, but is not all that plentiful, so look for the free car park sign in Winsford - it's near the inn.

Your walk starts at the inn and takes about an hour, leading over hilly, wooded terrain along bridle paths. Turn left as you leave the inn and walk a few yards up the hill until you see a well-defined path leading off to the left - it is waymarked Tarr Steps and Dulverton. After climbing along a steep rocky path for about 20 minutes you'll reach a gate, go through and turn left at the stream and cross the bridge. Turn left up the next hill and you'll soon reach a post indicating a bridleway to the right, and pointing back along the way you've come, but take the left track. Go through two gates and you'll see the sign Edbrooke/Summerway; turn left downhill to the road. Left again and follow the road for about ½mile to the village. On your right you'll pass the old village school where Ernest Bevin, Minister of Labour in Churchill's wartime government, began his education, and across the road on the left is the house (with a plaque) where he was born.
    When you reach the pub, don't go in immediately, but walk across the little packhorse bridge - Winsford has

at least eight bridges, maybe more, for that innocent-looking little stream – and go up the hill to the church of St Mary Magdalene. Notice when you get inside how the pillars on the south side of the nave slope outwards – this is thought to have been done to counteract a threatened collapse of the walls of the original Norman church while being enlarged in the 15th century. Look above the chancel arch at the windows on each side – they're reckoned to be rarities in church architecture in this part of the country. Look also at the door by which you entered – the ironwork is older than the wood, and dates back to the 13th century; it is thought to have come from Barlynch Priory, long since gone. Over the door opposite, the panel painted with the Royal Arms of James I, dates from 1609 and is one of only four known to be still in existence.

Return to the inn down the hill and by way of the small bridge over the River Exe.

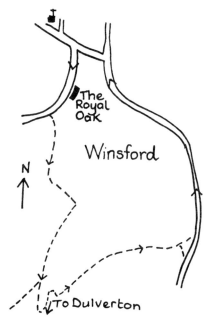